FIRST ESSAYS ON LITERATURE

FIRST ESSAYS ON LITERATURE

by

EDWARD SHANKS

Essay Index Reprint Series

 BOOKS FOR LIBRARIES PRESS

FREEPORT, NEW YORK

First Published 1923
Reprinted 1968

LIBRARY OF CONGRESS CATALOG CARD NUMBER:

68-20333

PRINTED IN THE UNITED STATES OF AMERICA

To
MONA AND CLENNEL WILKINSON

Preface

THE first ten essays in this collection are reprinted from the *London Mercury*. Of the remainder, five have appeared in the *New Statesman*, two in the *Saturday Westminster Gazette*, and one in the *Queen*. I am much indebted to the Editors of these journals.

All these essays have been revised since their first appearance in print. The earliest of them was written in 1917, the latest in the present year; and what I thought five years ago I do not necessarily think now. Where correction has seemed possible I have done my best to effect it—for in criticism surely, however it may be in poetry, early errors have no claim to be preserved, even as curiosities. It is as well to confess that in one instance I have gone so far as to convert a negative into an affirmative.

It is almost unnecessary to add that I should not dare to offer these studies of authors and books as illustrations of a definite principle of criticism. I should like to ask that they may be read as attempts to find such a principle. But literature is, strictly speaking, an impure form of activity. A definition of it, which does not include *Hamlet*, *The Decline and Fall of the Roman Empire*, *Roderick Hudson*, and *Kubla Khan*, or does not allow each of them to rank as excellent, involves a vicious simplification and is worse than useless. It is possible, no doubt, to base all one's judgments on a rigid theory of æsthetic, excluding all the other elements of what in ordinary speech we refer to as literature; but we can never prevent the mass of cultivated readers, to serve whom the critic exists, from being interested in these other elements. Nor can we prevent the mass of mankind from judging literature by some standard derived from outside it: for no man in the long run will ever admit the claim of literature to exist save in so far as it renders a service to him, however, consciously or unconsciously, he may define that service. The subjects which a critic must study are the psychology of mankind, with all its local, temporal, and accidental variations, and the successful practice of the great masters. And to deduce a simple general principle from this study might well be the work of a lifetime.

E. S.

Rodmell,
Sussex.

Contents

	PAGE
SAMUEL BUTLER	1
W. N. P. BARBELLION	23
THE LIFE OF GOETHE	46
THE POETRY OF MR. WALTER DE LA MARE	68
THE POETRY OF MR. JOHN FREEMAN	86
MR. MASEFIELD: SOME CHARACTERISTICS	104
MR. BELLOC: SOME CHARACTERISTICS	125
THE WORK OF MR. H. G. WELLS	148
REFLECTIONS ON THE RECENT HISTORY OF THE ENGLISH NOVEL	172
THE POSITION IN THE THEATRE	192
FOLK-SONG AS POETRY	207
THE SONNETS AND COMMON SENSE	215
SHELLEY AS A LYRIC POET	222
KEATS AND HIS CRITICS	229
THE LATER POETRY OF MR. W. B. YEATS	238
W. E. HENLEY	245
MR. RABINDRANATH TAGORE	253
SWEET BODEMENTS	258

Samuel Butler[1]

SAMUEL BUTLER was a philosopher whose favourite doctrine was expressed in the words *pas trop de zèle*; and he spent a great part of his life complaining a little too eagerly that the world was not sufficiently zealous in appreciation of his works. His reception and his reputation did indeed deserve a considerable part of the almost excessive attention which he lavished on them; for at this moment, now that the first is accomplished and the second enormous, they make a very curious subject for study. In his notebooks they occur again and again as themes for his meditation. " I am the *enfant terrible*," he says, " of literature and science. If I cannot, and I know I cannot, get the literary and scientific big-wigs to give me a shilling, I can, and I know I can, heave bricks into the middle of them." " I have chosen the fighting-road," he says elsewhere, " rather than the hang-on-to-a-great-man road, and what can a man who does this look for except that people should try to silence him in whatever way they think will be most effectual ? In my case they have thought it best to pretend that I am non-existent." There is something pathetic in the spectacle of a man pursuing " the fighting-road " with no one to fight him and heaving bricks into the middle of persons who obstinately continue to ignore his existence. There is something more pathetic in the spectacle of an original thinker and a great wit sitting down in isolation to pen these apologies for his obscure

[1] *Samuel Butler : a Memoir.* By H. Festing Jones. 2 vols. (Macmillan.)

position, always affecting to be indifferent to it and never deceiving any one. For Butler was not indifferent to his lack of success. Had his been a true and not an assumed indifference he could not have returned to the subject so often as he does and in so many keys. He betrays himself again and again beyond mistake. He was an intensely, a morbidly sensitive man, one to whom success would have been very pleasant. He was damaged, and confirmed in oddity, by the want of it. He missed it because of what first started him in oddity—that is to say, an unfortunate childhood.

"The subject of this memoir," so Butler once suggested that his biography ought to begin, "was the son of rich but dishonest parents." Dishonest they may have been: respectable they certainly were. Dr. Butler, the first distinguished member of the family, was for twenty-seven years head master of Shrewsbury, a man with all the attributes of the great schoolmasters of the early nineteenth century, an imposing figure, who, towards the end of his life, became Bishop of Lichfield. His son was not so distinguished. His sole claim to be remembered, if his canonry be disregarded, is the fact that somehow or other he became the father of 'Erewhon' Butler. There is much detail in Mr. Festing Jones's enormous book on Butler's early life and his relation to his parents; but there is nothing quite so significant as an anecdote which occurs in the second volume:—

"At Saas he made the acquaintance of Mr. and Mrs. MacCarthy, who were staying in the hotel with their son, an Eton boy. One day the father and son had been for an excursion and the

father returned alone. The anxious mother, hearing
that her boy preferred speculating in short cuts to
accompanying his father, borrowed a red umbrella
to make herself conspicuous, and went out ' to look
for Desmond.' Presently she came upon Butler
loaded up with his camera and toiling along on
his way back after a fatiguing day. He told her
he had seen a little white figure among the trees
on the mountain-side and had no doubt it was her
son who, he assured her, would be all right, and
he himself was loitering, intending to be overtaken so that they might arrive at the hotel together.

" ' You see,' he explained, ' I know he will be
late for dinner and it may make things a little
easier for him if he does not come in alone.'

" Years afterwards Mrs. MacCarthy told me
that she had been reading *The Way of All Flesh*,
and had remembered this incident and for the
first time had understood why Butler thought that
her son would require the presence of an elderly
gentleman to protect him from his parents if he
came in late for dinner."

This throws a curious and unexpected sidelight
on Butler's childhood, from the effects of which he
never recovered. His parents learnt the art of
bringing up children from a book which adjured
them to " Break your child's will early or he will
break yours later on." They did not break it,
but unquestionably they deformed it. This may
have been done on principle. To Butler, however, it sometimes seemed to spring from other
motives. " I have felt," he once said of his father,
" that he has always looked upon me as something
which he could badger with impunity." He said
that, like Ernest Pontifex, with regard to his

3

father he could remember no feeling during his childhood except fear and shrinking.

Nor was this life of terror and pain lightened by any gracious or liberal influences. The world which Mr. Festing Jones exhibits to us in his opening chapters is full of the drabbest and most depressing horrors of Early Victorianism. Its measure can be taken by a single story which Butler preserved:—

" Archdeacon Bather was lunching with my grandfather some two or three years after the Archdeacon had lost his first wife. Dr. Butler dearly loved a hard crust of bread baked nearly black, and it so happened that a piece was set by his plate with hardly any crust, and what little there was very thin. My aunt, then Miss Butler, observing what had happened, at once said:—

" ' Oh, papa, this won't do at all, I will find you a piece more to your liking.' Whereon she went to the kitchen, and returned with a crust baked exactly to Dr. Butler's taste.

"When the Archdeacon saw this he said to himself: 'That is the young woman for me'; and shortly afterwards he proposed and was accepted."

Readers will remember the scene in *The Way of All Flesh* in which Theobald, driving away for his honeymoon, insists that Christina shall order their dinner at the first stop, and in which Christina protests with tears her nervousness, and Theobald replies, " It is a wife's duty to order her husband's dinner; you are my wife, and I shall expect you to order mine." A sensitive child, neglected or

4

even ill-treated by his parents, might, if the relations of the parents between themselves had anything beautiful or kindly, see some possibilities of happiness in the institution of the family. But Samuel Butler was brought up in a world where no such possibilities seemed to exist. He came to believe, Mr. Festing Jones tells us, that, like Habakkuk, *le père de famille est capable de tout.* It has often been maintained that the greatest poets and artists do nothing throughout life but draw on those fresh and lovely impressions which they have gathered in childhood. When he was a child Butler acquired habits of suspicion against all those surrounding him who were not connected with him by freely-chosen bonds of friendship. Canon Butler bullied him on moral grounds; and he grew to suspect every claim made on him, every exhortation addressed to him, on moral grounds. Ernest Pontifex is described on one occasion as assuming the expression of a puppy which is being scolded for something it does not understand; and Butler did indeed develop some of the habits of an ill-treated dog. He shied and snarled at a lifted hand, which might have been lifted in kindness or in ignorance of his existence. Having, as he supposed, penetrated the fraud of the family, he felt a distrust of all human institutions. He suspected the world of being in a conspiracy to pretend that parents were naturally kind to their children, that Christ rose from the dead, and that Tennyson was a great poet. And, turning from all these discredited shows, he devoted himself in isolation to the care of his own idiosyncrasies and the companionship of a very few, very intimate friends.

Here, where in one case he might have suspected with justice, he was all blind trust. The story of Charles Paine Pauli is one of the most extraordinary that have been brought to light in human records in recent years. A correspondent who knew this man and admired him wrote not long ago to *The Times*, not to controvert Mr. Festing Jones's account of the relations between him and Butler, but to protest, in an almost agonised manner, that there must be some explanation of it; and this is precisely what the reader, who did not know Pauli, feels when he comes upon these pages. But there seems to be no explanation.

In 1859 Butler rebelled against his father, and finally decided that he could not take Orders, basing his refusal on " doubts," which in after years seemed to him no less absurd than the doctrines against which they were directed. As a result of this he emigrated to New Zealand, taking with him an allowance from Canon Butler and a promise of support in capital, in order that he might establish himself as a sheep-farmer. In this occupation he was, against all the probabilities, moderately successful, and, largely owing to the rapidly-developing condition of the colony, managed to turn an original capital of £4400 into the sum of £8000. But finding this life uncongenial, he concluded that it would be wiser to invest his money in New Zealand, where the current rate of interest was 10 per cent., and go home and live on the proceeds. While he was making preparations to this end, a previous slight acquaintance with Pauli developed into an intimate friendship. Pauli was handsome, fascinating, well-dressed, ineffably well-mannered. He was, in fact, the Towneley of *The Way of All Flesh*, though Providence, not doing as well by him as by Towneley, had omitted to make him rich. He was actually poor and in ill-health, and anxious to go to England in order that he might recover. He then proposed to get called to the Bar and to return to New Zealand to practise. Butler, who believed himself to be worth about £800 a year, promptly lavished on this creature the generosity and tenderness which had found no outlet during his childhood. He offered to lend him £100 for his passage and to allow him £200 a year for three years—that is, until his return to New Zealand as a barrister. They accordingly made the passage together ; and Butler kept his promise, and more than kept it, extending the allowance, even through the time of his acutest financial difficulties, until Pauli's death in 1897. It was then discovered that Pauli had been earning £900 a year, and that even at the last he earned between £500 and £700. He left a fortune of £9000; but Butler was not mentioned in the will and received his invitation to the funeral by way of the undertaker.

A singular and enlightening circumstance in the intercourse between Butler and Pauli unhappily prevents Mr. Festing Jones from making this astonishing but veracious narrative entirely lifelike. The charming young man did not reciprocate the feelings of his pathetic and somewhat uncouth adorer. " I had felt from the very beginning," says Butler, " that my intimacy with Pauli was only superficial, and I also perceived more and more that I bored him." Pauli confessed that he had never been more miserable in his life than once when he spent a holiday with Butler at Dieppe. Consequently it soon came about that the essential part of the relations between

7

them was the punctual payment of the allowance. Latterly, they met only three times a week, when Pauli lunched in Butler's chambers. He discontinued informing Butler of his changes of address, so that at the end Butler did not know where he was living, and Mr. Festing Jones met him " only on business, for he would have nothing to do with any of Butler's friends in any other way." Butler learnt of his death from an announcement in *The Times*.

Truly a mysterious creature! And his friend is very comprehensible in supposing that there must be some explanation. Possibly Mr. Festing Jones, if he had met him otherwise than purely on business, might have given us some impression of his personality which would have let in light on this dark business. As it is, we must content ourselves with wonder at the extraordinary situations which human nature is capable of creating. But this unhappy friendship is worth examining, apart from its intrinsic curiosity, because it presents in extremity an essential and determining part of Butler's life. His devotion and loyalty to his friends were perhaps the most beautiful things in his character and do much to redeem his somewhat unlovely attitude of snarling and suspicion towards all strangers.

Life might have been thought to have treated him savagely in following up his parents with the hardly less cruel Pauli. He disguised the shock of his discovery on Pauli's death by remarking that he would now save not only £200 a year, but also the cost of those three lunches a week in Clifford's Inn. Yet a nature that opened itself so trustingly, so defencelessly, must have suffered on finding its bounty abused. But in his other friends, in

Miss Savage, in his clerk, Alfred Emery Cathie, and in Mr. Festing Jones he had ample compensations. He was a man who at first sight was not readily liked. He was awkward and nervous in the company of strangers, and it is likely that he did not disguise so well as he supposed his grave misgivings that they were either pretentious scoundrels or conceited hypocrites. He was always badly and carelessly dressed; and though his portraits, when one is used to them and can associate them with the best one knows of his mind, become attractive, there can be no denial that his appearance was on the most lenient showing decidedly grotesque, that of a difficult, taciturn, maliciously observant gnome, roughly carved in a hard wood. It took some time and some degree of intuition to penetrate behind this mask. Those who did so were rewarded and rewarded him. Miss Savage, who used to meet him first at Heatherley's art-classes, was not attracted by him for a considerable time. When at last she was, it was by a flash of remarkable intuition. In commenting on one of his books, she writes:—

" I like the cherry-eating scene, too, because it reminded me of your eating cherries when first I knew you. One day when I was going to the gallery, a very hot day, I remember, I met you on the shady side of Berners Street eating cherries out of a basket. Like your Italian friends, you were perfectly silent with content, and you handed the basket to me as I was passing, without saying a word. I pulled out a handful and went on my way rejoicing, without saying a word either. I had not before perceived you to be different from any one else."

9

It is not certain whether Miss Savage became a Butlerian or whether Butler acquired something of what we consider his characteristic attitude of mind from her. If he did not, then her spirit leapt at once to answer his as soon as she had perceived the possibility of common interests between them, for her first letters to him are written in his own vein. She entered immediately into his concerns, read all his books in manuscript, criticised them, gave them more praise than they received from any one else, and abused his enemies with a gusto equal to his. The only trouble between them in their long connection was his gnawing fear that she wanted to marry him. And he did not want to marry any one, let alone her who was—

" Plain and lame and fat and short,
Forty and overkind."

But if all these disabilities had been removed, he would still have been disinclined to marry her. He did not believe in marriage, had a hatred of the family ; and he slunk snarling away from the danger like a terror-stricken wild animal at the sight of a trap, only to reproach himself in after years for unkindness to his friend. But his relations with women were not, and he did not intend that they should be, of the sort that leads to marriage. He had mistresses, whom he visited. Mr. J. B. Yeats, in a recent paper of reminiscences, has repeated his avowals on this point in a manner which conveys well enough Butler's view that his lapses were caused by a necessity of the flesh. One of his mistresses, referred to as " Madame," was after a long connection allowed to visit his chambers in Clifford's Inn. No other gained this privilege; and Butler extended it to her as he might have done to an old and well-tried servant. Butler did not love these women, he frequented them. He was almost insensible to the notion that there might be anything beautiful in the relations between the sexes, as he was insensible to the notion that there might be anything of value written in verse. Theobald and Christina pretended to like poetry: Theobald and Christina pretended to love one another and him. It was all of a piece with their pretence that Christianity was a religion of kindliness and enlightenment.

So he remained a bachelor, and, when Miss Savage was dead, contented himself with the intimate companionship of Mr. Jones and Alfred, his clerk. After he had resigned the ambition of becoming a painter, after his odd and disastrous excursion into the world of business, his daily life was that of an eccentric gentleman with a small independent income. He read and wrote in the British Museum, he went for walks in the country and took holidays in Italy, he published his books at his own expense, and he scrambled out of invitations to dinner as best he could. For a hobby he wrote music in collaboration with Mr. Festing Jones, oratorios which were to be as much like Handel's oratorios as possible. The first of them, *Narcissus*, was inspired by his own misfortunes in business, and the final chorus ran:—

" How blest the prudent man, the maiden pure,
Whose income is both ample and secure,
Arising from consolidated Three
Per Cent. Annuities, paid quarterly! "

" We remembered Handel's treatment of ' continually,' " says Mr. Festing Jones, " and thought we could not do better than imitate it for our words ' paid quarterly.' "

And so his life went on and his interests drifted through the theory of evolution, the authorship of the *Odyssey*, the life of his grandfather, and the meaning of Shakespeare's Sonnets. The sales of his books pursued a course by no means so varied, but steadily declined. In 1899, when he drew up a statement of profit and loss, the average sales of his eleven books, excluding *Erewhon*, which was the first, amounted to 306 copies each. Of his *Selections from Previous Works*, 120 copies were sold in fifteen years. Of the *Authoress of the Odyssey*, 165 copies were sold. He might well have added discouragement to his first cause of bitterness. The religion of Christ produced Canon Butler, the religion of science produced Darwin, the religion of good looks and good breeding produced Pauli. On paper he was indomitable. He swore he had enjoyed life, that on the balance his good luck had exceeded the bad. But he swore a little too often, he explained a little too much in detail, for this to have been quite true. And then, at the very end of his life, the luck turned, and his last book, by a strange irony, was produced at the publisher's own risk, the greatest triumph in his literary career which he had been able to attain since the success of his first. After he was dead his reputation, magically assisted with incantations by Mr. Bernard Shaw and others, sprang up to an amazing height, like the plant grown from the Indian enchanter's bean.

Now the world is confronted with a situation in which the neglected philosopher of Clifford's Inn has attained an importance he never dreamt of and perhaps would not have approved. " Above

all things," he said, " let no unwary reader do me
the injustice of believing in *me*." This useful
motto was printed on the menu of the first Erewhon
dinner; but a great number of his disciples have
disregarded the admonition. I was once the
witness of one undergraduate trying to proselytise
another and telling him that it was a worthy ambition
to desire to be like Christ. " I don't want to be
like any one else," replied the second undergraduate, " but if I did, I shouldn't choose Christ,
I should choose Samuel Butler." This is at once
an extreme instance and one strictly guarded against
Butler's own disapproval: for the kernel of the
remark would meet with his applause. But it
illustrates the direction in which many of his
admirers have more frenetically rushed. It is an
ironic fate for so ironic a philosopher that his
teaching should have become a sort of Tom Tiddler's
ground for so many solemn and ridiculous persons.

What, after all, is his total achievement ? He
himself summed up what he considered to be his
life-work in a statement which is not dated but
which must have been written in 1899 or later.
It begins with (1) The emphasising the analogies
between crime and disease (*Erewhon*), and ends
with (17) The elucidation of Shakespeare's *Sonnets*
(*Shakespeare's Sonnets Reconsidered*). " The fore-
going," he contiuues, " is the list of my mares'-
nests, and it is, I presume, this list which made
Mr. Arthur Platt call me the Galileo of mares'-
nests in his diatribe on my *Odyssey* theory in the
Classical Review." The two to which he probably
attached most importance, to judge from the
bitterness of his remarks on their reception, were
his intervention into the great evolution dispute
and his great discovery that the *Odyssey* was written

by a female inhabitant of Trapani in Sicily. With
regard to the second he continually complained
that no classical scholar had ever replied to his
arguments. It was once remarked in answer to
this, that if a classical scholar published a book
arguing that no player of Rugby football ought to
be allowed to pass the ball without obtaining a
signed receipt for it, the great community of Rugby
footballers, intent on other matters, would probably
ignore his suggestion. Butler's claim may perhaps
be left there. Yet he did apparently take it
seriously, in spite of his failure to deal with the
singular fact that no scrap of confirmation of his
theory has survived from the writings or the
traditions of antiquity. His " mares'-nests," he
said, " were simply sovereigns which he found
lying in public places and which people would not
notice and be at the trouble of picking up." They
were mostly, however, one cannot help suspecting,
recommended to him less because they seemed to
be sovereigns than because other people would
not pick them up. They were, in fact, the notions
of a crank, who, having acquired a distrust of the
rest of the world, took pains to differ from it as
much as he could.

His theories of evolution hold a different position.
Darwin's theory has now been so greatly modified,
as much by his supporters as by his opponents,
that it cannot be said any longer to hold the field
as he first presented it; and Butler's attitude has
been largely justified. But this change has been
accomplished less by the acceptance of Butler's
views than by the work of experimental biologists.
He did, in fact, offer several general principles,
many well-founded, some mistaken, all stimulating,
for the consideration of practical workers; and it

14

is not possible to overlook the fact that his writings have had considerable influence on the development of science. But Charles Darwin and his followers were practical men—men no doubt with faults, with the intolerance and impatience of the laity that are often to be found in the scientific investigator. It is not hard to see why they received Butler with tepid interest, and finally ignored him when he forsook their path of inquiry. For they did ignore him: they did not, as he supposed, conspire to silence him. He seems to have believed that Darwin was a sort of Anti-Christ malevolently determined to force on humanity a diabolical belief of his own invention; and he was only too ready to suspect him of unscrupulous dealing and machinations. When he conceived that Darwin had engineered an attack on him, though he obtained an expression of regret for an accident, he flung violently into print, and did, though he remained ignorant of the fact, get from Darwin and his friends the attention as an enemy which they would not bestow on him as a friendly critic. His letter to the *Athenæum* seriously perturbed Darwin, who drafted two replies to it, and submitted them for advice to the members of his family and to Professor Huxley. The advice given was against replying; and Butler was accordingly confirmed in his opinion. But this was an opinion which a less suspicious man would have been slower in forming and less stubborn in holding.

Darwin was not, in his career or in his handling of Butler, a model of the urbane virtues. Butler did right to protest against the sacerdotal attitude which Victorian men of science frequently adopted. But he did wrong not to realise that Darwin did not take him altogether seriously, and why this was so. Butler's challenging manner of writing, the prickly defensiveness which he developed on the smallest provocation, must have been disagreeable to the great investigator who had spent years of careful research into the problems which, he thought, Butler airily settled at his writing-table in the intervals of other pursuits. Darwin is perhaps to blame, but not so greatly to blame as Butler contended, if he regarded Butler at first as a well-disposed, and then as an ill-disposed, amateur; and that was in effect his view of the whole matter. When he sent *Evolution Old and New* to Dr. Krause, he expressed the hope that the German writer " would not expend much powder and shot on Mr. Butler, for he really is not worthy of it. His book is merely ephemeral." It was characteristic of the professional scientist to dismiss thus slightingly what was not founded on actual observation and practical experiment. Butler's reply was that he took his facts from those who made it their business to collect facts : these were the very people who were now attacking him, but surely they did not attack the accuracy of his data. The reply seems to be valid. But Darwin's inability to see it was due less to malignity than to a kind of myopia which often afflicts the experimental scientist.

Some of Butler's " mares'-nests," then, were " mares'-nests " from the beginning. Others, neglected when they might have been useful, have begun to lose interest now that they have been confirmed and carried further by practical work. But he remains, apart from his theories and his discoveries, as an observer of life and a teacher of conduct. Passages of this nature exist in all his works; but, generally speaking, his claim to be accepted as a

16

philosopher rests on five books, *Erewhon*, *Erewhon Revisited*, the *Note-books*, *The Way of All Flesh*, and Mr. Festing Jones's biography.

Mr. Festing Jones observes that " I was struck by his uncompromising sincerity. If a subject interested him, he took infinite pains to find out all he could about it at first-hand, thought it over and formed an opinion of his own, without reference to what any one else thought or said." In demonstration of this, Mr. Jones relates the following reminiscences:—

" We talked about Charlotte Brontë; Butler did not like her; I said, as though taking the odd trick with the ace of trumps:—

" ' Well, at all events, she wrote three splendid novels.'

" He replied in a low voice, reluctantly but decidedly: ' They are not splendid.'

" These four words shifted the subject under discussion from the splendour or otherwise of Charlotte Brontë's novels to the sincerity or otherwise of my opinion."

It was no doubt well that Mr. Jones's sincerity should be probed; and this is in fact what Butler does at his best. He challenges established opinions and forces those who hold them to consider whether they have any good ground for doing so. But the reader who is not dazzled by Butler's originality of judgment in this instance will ask himself whether the sentence which Mr. Jones quotes is anything more than a very facile assertion. He will then perhaps ask himself how often Butler's original pronouncements on established reputations are of the same order. He will certainly find some that are not. In the *Note-books* there is an elaborate arraignment of Raphael. It may not be convincing; but the critic has produced his arguments. Here, also, may be found Butler's explanation of his hostility towards post-Handelian music. But one may search the two volumes of the biography for a considerable time without finding his appreciation of any book published in his own time. Here, again, we must be just: Butler did like one book. It was called *Pusley, or My Summer in a Garden*; its author was Charles Dudley Warner; and Butler said, " I like *Pusley* very much and have read it all."

But the majority of his opinions are on the model of the much-quoted passage in the *Note-books*:—

" Talking it over, we agreed that Blake was no good because he learnt Italian at over sixty in order to read Dante, and we knew Dante was no good because he was so fond of Virgil, and Virgil was no good because Tennyson ran him, and as for Tennyson—well, Tennyson goes without saying."

That is an exceedingly witty way of expressing an indolent prejudice; and those who share that particular chain of prejudices may well rejoice in it, without supposing that it proves their case. But this particular form of humour grows wearisome; and Butler's independence of attitude would be slightly more entertaining and useful if he had occasionally replaced the reputations he smashed with these hammer-strokes by some discovery of his own. Unfortunately, it is not easy to remember any unknown author whom he brought into the light—unless Nausicaa be taken as such.

18

But this is, in a way, the defect of his qualities. It is easy, too easy, to grow incensed with him when he inanely doubts any convention or opinion that comes in sight. It is possible to remark of him, adapting the remark made of Dr. Johnson, that he may have been very sensible at bottom, but that there was a great deal of nonsense on top. But the fact remains that by challenging everything he did detect many frauds, and he did let the light of scepticism into many topics where scepticism is a healthy attitude. If his view of family life was bigoted and unreasonable, there is a great deal of use in the reminder that family life is not necessarily perfect and needs a deal of watching to keep it from being very imperfect indeed. Some of the assumptions he challenged have now disappeared. We no longer believe that good looks and good manners are the unmistakable indices of an ill heart; and we are becoming convinced that it is better to have these attributes than to be without them. But these lessons may still with advantage be enforced as Butler continually enforces them. It was his fate that life made him a suspicious man. But suspicion made him a doubting, questioning, and therefore inquiring man. And his natural gift of humour taught him what he has ever since been teaching others, that it is possible to be serious without being solemn. This was perhaps the most valuable thing he had to say to a society emerging from the Victorian era and passing over into another that was to be as desperately serious as we are now realising. It is a reflection pathetically ironical that some of his loudest followers in these days should be persons whom he would very likely have described as Simeonites of the intellect.

First Essays on Literature

Of the value of his writings judged as literature it is not so easy to speak with confidence. *Erewhon* is not so much a novel as a collection of essays roughly pressed into a common mould. They are not merely disconnected, they are also composed on different planes of satire, at different removes from reality, so that the reader as he goes from chapter to chapter has an uncomfortable sense of being jolted from level to level. Yet the satire, on its varying levels, is extraordinarily easy, ingenious and penetrating; and, in another key again, the opening chapters make one of the best introductions to a story of exploration ever written. *Erewhon Revisited* is the book of an old man; and it has much of the beauty so often to be found in such compositions. The manner of its writing was very different from that of its predecessor, and it is impossible to complain of any unevenness in its structure. Nevertheless, the satire is not so easy. It is a little strained, a little too ingenious, a little too closely calculated to make good reading. Butler himself picked out the best part of the book when he complained that none of his critics had noticed the idea of a father attempting by noble conduct to deserve the good opinion of a newly-found and adored son. Thus, at the end of his life, still haunted by early memories, he attempted to fashion in imagination what should have been and completely to invert the facts of his own childhood.

The Way of All Flesh is precisely the opposite of this. It has long been known to be of the photographic order of novels; but how minutely photographic it is we could not know until the appearance of Mr. Jones's book. This need not, and should not, affect our judgment of it, even when we are

20

informed that Theobald's delightful letters are
almost literal transcriptions from those of Canon
Butler. We can very well continue to admire the
inimitable accuracy and vividness with which these
real scenes are described, while we suffer from the
painful bitterness of this exhaustive improvisation
on the old theme of parents and children. But the
whole book is not of equal merit. It begins to
weaken at the point where Ernest's career diverges
from Butler's own experience; and when it reaches
the catastrophe it sinks into improbabilities from
which it never recovers. The Ernest, whose
thoughts and feelings at Cambridge have been
described, and who was Butler, would never have
made that disastrous mistake over Miss Maitland's
real profession. Butler did not, in fact, ever make
it, nor did he ever develop into the super-prig
which Ernest became after his release from prison.

Butler's reputation will probably rest more and
more, as time goes on, on his *Note-books* and on
Mr. Jones's biography, which might be described
together as the story of a distrustful man. Indeed,
posterity, reading these alone, will probably miss
little of what it should retain: for Butler was careful
of his best things, and most of them are to be found
here as well as in the books in which he enshrined
them among more perishable material. On the
strength of these two books he will remain a definite
and unforgettable character, though he may, probably will, recede in importance, perhaps even to
the level of those wits whose " table-talk " is read
by the curious in every generation.

But even so, there he will be still: a man whom
fate tortured into such distrust of his fellows as
to make him question everything and teach others
to do the same. He suffered intensely in the process

21

that made him what he was: he suffered again, much more than he would ever admit, from the ineffaceable results of the process. " I do not deny, however," he bursts out, " that I have been ill-used. I have been used abominably." This cry rings truer, echoes longer in the memory, than the assertion which follows that he considered the balance of good fortune to have been on his side. By one of those contrivances of events with which fate marks the lives of distinguished men, an atmosphere of distrust followed him on to his death-bed and beyond it. For the doctors disagreed during his last illness, and Mr. Festing Jones doubts the accuracy of the causes given in the certificate of death.

W. N. P. Barbellion [1]

WHEN *The Journal of a Disappointed Man* was first published in March, 1919, the suspicious circumstances that it contained an introduction by Mr. H. G. Wells, and purported to be written by a young assistant in the Natural History Museum at South Kensington, immediately produced the impression that it was a fictitious work, composed by Mr. Wells himself. He was known at that time, from other books acknowledged to be his, to be feeling a particular interest in the philosophical problem of human suffering; he had done something of the kind before, and many readers, it may be conjectured, unconsciously found it a relief to suppose that this almost unbearably tragic history had been invented. But the impression could not long survive a careful study of the book. The author's identity was soon guessed at by a few persons who knew him and suspected by some who had heard of him; and presently Mr. Wells wrote to a newspaper to say that the only fictitious details in the Journal were the author's name and the date of his death, there given as December 31st, 1917. This date was in fact incorrect by nearly two years. Bruce Frederick Cummings lived until October 30th, 1919, that is to say, for seven months after the publication of his diary.

Thus it comes about that the later part of it, which has recently been printed, contains many references to his critics, in whose opinions he was deeply and frankly interested. He remarks again

[1] *The Journal of a Disappointed Man. Enjoying Life and Other Essays.* By W. N. P. Barbellion. (Chatto and Windus.)

23

and again on the ordinary incompetence of reviewers, the usual complaint of an author, but especially poignant here. He mentions, once in a letter and once in the diary, an imbecile who thought that he was a " social climber "; and he welcomes with joy the first writer who seemed to him to have read the book carefully. But among all these references to his work there is none more illuminating than the last entry he ever made:—

" Friends and relatives say I have not drawn my true self. But that's because I have taken my clothes off and they can't recognise me stark! The Book is a self-portrait in the nude."

Thus, with this final self-explanation, he ends his work. The last two words stand alone at the top of a left-hand page, and opposite them in the book lies the blotting paper he used. He had often before said farewell to his Journal. Once it was in a fit of disgust with it and himself, and he took it up again to record the discovery that he was suffering from an incurable disease. Then, owing to the paralysis of his right hand, writing became too painful for him, and he thought this the hardest and shrewdest stroke of fate, to deprive him of his secret consolation. Last, under the date May 25th, 1919, he made an entry of four pages, chiefly supplementing earlier entries, and concluded with the words large and scrawled, but legible: " This is the end. I am not going to keep a diary any more." But on June 1st, without explanation, he made a long entry, recalling an experience of early life, and on June 3rd the very last, which I have quoted.[1] He desired that at the end should be

[1] These entries do not appear in this order in the published book. *The Last Diary* was written deliberately as a literary composition

written, "The rest is silence," to serve as an inscription on the base of his " self-erected monument." Genuine self-portraits in the nude occur very rarely in the history of literature. This is a picture of a man of genius vividly drawn by himself. It is a remarkable book about a remarkable man.

Barbellion was born on September 7th, 1889, and was the third son of a reporter on a newspaper in a Devonshire town. He was able to remember the first time a bird's nest was ever shown to him; but a passion for natural history became very early the most important part of his life. He was articled as a boy to his father's unattractive and uncongenial profession. He nevertheless continued to pursue his passion with an extraordinary energy and strength of will, and was determined to secure somehow or other an entrance into the desired career. He was otherwise and exactingly occupied and he was entirely self-taught; and in 1910, just when by great good fortune he had been offered, and had accepted, a post in the Plymouth Marine Laboratory, his father's health broke down altogether, compelling him to renounce this dazzling but ill-paid opportunity. But in the following year he won in open competition an appointment in the Natural History Museum, which justified the abandonment of journalism.

In 1909 there first appears in the diary the definite indication of a theme which was soon to rival natural history in importance and at last most horribly to overwhelm it.

for publication. The manuscript contains directions that certain passages shall be removed from their strictly chronological places and inserted elsewhere.

" Feeling ill—like a sloppy tadpole. My will is paralysed. I visit the Doctor regularly to be stethoscoped, ramble about the streets, idly scan magazines in the Library and occasionally rink— with palpitation of the heart as a consequence. In view of the shortness, bitterness, and uncertainty of life, all scientific labour for me seems futile."

After this he does not often forget the subject of his health for many pages together. The deaths of his father and mother deepened the preoccupation, and Barbellion's symptoms and dreads were almost infinite in their variety. He suffered from intermittent action of the heart, from nervous weakness, and from dyspepsia; he feared now paralysis, now blindness, now consumption. The thought of death was constantly with him, but until the end he could not be sure in what form it would come. Sometimes he demanded that it should finish his sufferings, sometimes he hoped it would delay a little more to allow him to complete the work he had in hand.

Meanwhile, amid the unescapable and agonising reflections which this condition induced, another side of his nature was being developed. In 1910 there is an entry which, again, is like the first tentative introduction of a musical theme in a symphony:—

" I hope to goodness she doesn't think I want to marry her. In the Park, in the dark, kissing her, I was testing and experimenting with a new experience."

He was not, of course, by any means so callous and inhuman as this brief note might make him appear;

but he was immensely curious about himself and about other people, and immensely greedy for new sensations. He dabbled a good deal in love-making, and his dabbling was prompted as much by curiosity as by the natural pressure of the senses. At last he fell in love, could not make up his mind whether he wanted to marry, made it up and was rejected, felt relieved, then unhappy, renewed his suit and was accepted. In September, 1915, he was married. A few weeks before, during a holiday at Coniston, boisterously prosecuted with his usual reckless disregard of his weak health, he had fallen and jarred his spine, and this had brought on a partial paralysis which filled him with the gloomiest thoughts and seemed to suggest the cancellation of all his plans. But his doctor made light of the matter and the marriage took place.

In the following November, having formally presented himself for recruitment, he was led by curiosity to read the sealed certificate written by his own doctor, not supposing that its being sealed had any particular meaning. Thus he discovered, while sitting in a railway-carriage, that eighteen months before he had shown the first symptoms of a terrible and incurable disease and that this had been concealed from him, though it had been communicated to his relatives. He found later that his wife had learnt of it before their marriage, and also that his fall at Coniston had reawakened activity among the bacteria and hastened the end. In 1916 his daughter was born, and in July of the following year his rapidly failing strength compelled him, after ineffectual periods of sick leave, to resign his appointment at the Museum. His health varied; he grew worse and recovered a little,

27

but never recovered what he had lost. He prepared his diary for publication, but the publishers who had first accepted it became afraid of it when it was partly set up in type and asked to be relieved of the undertaking. Another publisher was found. The book appeared, and its reception did something to soften the miseries of his last months.

How profound and unremitting were these miseries, and how he bore them, is shown in the last section of the diary. His disease was painful and the end certain. He had a wife who was often fatigued and ill, and a child, and he had next to no money. The strain of witnessing his sufferings, as well as the necessity of earning her living, made it imperative that his wife should spend long periods of time away from him. In 1919 there was an idea that a certain prolonged and troublesome treatment might possibly, though only possibly, effect an improvement. But he did not care to be experimented with then. He was already dead, he said, and it was too late, he could not bear the burden of a fresh hope. He continued to be tortured by the long-drawn-out agony of his dissolution, by the defeat of all his ambitions, and by the black prospects of his wife and child. But the success of his book brings a curiously sweeter and gentle note into the diary, a note most poignant to the reader who could understand his refusing to be grateful for anything.

" I am still miserable " (he writes), " especially on E.'s account—that dear, brave woman. But I have suffered a *change*. My whole soul is sweetened by the love of those near and dear to me, and by the sympathy of those reading my book."

Grants were made to him out of various funds, and, just before his death, a committee of distinguished literary men was formed to see that his wife and child did not want. This in particular touched him to gratitude, and he died proud and happy in the thought that those who should have been dependent on him had so many good friends to serve them instead. A few hours before his death he said to his brother, " You will soon be able to blow the trumpets and bang the brasses "; but his eyes were full of a pathetic desire to have it denied.

It is not difficult to understand the complaint made by his friends and relatives that he had drawn a misleading portrait of himself, any more than it is difficult to understand his own protest that he had drawn himself with the clothes off. Both points of view are exceedingly natural, and perhaps it is possible for a disinterested observer to see in the diary the whole truth which could not be immediately obvious either to himself or to those who were closely connected with him. We need not involve ourselves very deeply in the theories of psycho-analysis to make the point that a man who keeps a journal of this sort probably does so because there is something in him which ordinary life keeps under, which he desires to express and cannot, except thus in secret. Hence come apparent contradictions between the outward appearance and the confession. On one occasion Barbellion says:—

" I have no personal courage and all this pride boils up behind a timid exterior. I quail often before stupid but overbearing persons who consequently never realise my contempt of them. . . . Of course, to intimate friends (only about three persons in the wide, wide world), I can always give free vent to my feelings, and I do so in privacy with that violence in which a weak character usually finds some compensation for his intolerable self-imposed reserve and restraint in public. I can never marvel enough at the ineradicable turpitude of my existence, at my *double-facedness*, and the remarkable contrast between the face I turn to the outside world and the face my friends know. It's like leading a double existence or artificially constructing a puppet to dangle before the crowd while I fulminate behind the scenes. If only I had the moral courage to play my part in life—to take the stage and be myself, to enjoy the delightful sensation of making my presence felt, instead of this vapourish mumming—then this Journal would be quite unnecessary."

No man who is a hero to himself stands a very good chance of seeming a hero to other people. But in this passage Barbellion not only shows the difference between his appearance and his self-portraiture, but also directs attention to one of the factors which make his diary so interesting a document. He was aware of the contrast between what he allowed the world to see and the rest of his nature; but this contrast remained profoundly mysterious to himself. He understood himself enough to be able to describe himself, but not so thoroughly that the knowledge could remove all curiosity; and, in fact, while he knew much of his own character that no one else knew, there was something left over of which he was ignorant.

He once said:—

" I am apparently a triple personality: (1) The

respectable youth; (2) The foul-mouthed commen-
tator and critic ; (3) The real but unknown I.
Curious that these three should live together amiably
in the same tenement."

One might also say that the reader of the diary
discovers another triple personality: (1) Barbellion
as he must have seemed to others; (2) Barbellion
as he thought he seemed to others; (3) The real
Barbellion, not fully known even to himself, yet,
between his appearance and his confessions, for
ever unconsciously betraying himself. In actual
fact, he was, it is agreed by all who knew him, a
man of tremendous, almost dæmonic, force of
character. I have already alluded to the restless
vigour with which he drove his failing body through
all manner of tasks and difficulties, and this trait
in him gives a fair idea of his spirit. From boy-
hood onward he was weakened by continual ill-
health. The diary is full of medical observations
and forebodings, but no one, not even his family,
realised how constantly the fear of sickness and
death attended him. He never mentioned his
health save in a tone of cheerful cynicism: he never
pampered himself or allowed himself to be pampered. In spite of his palpitating heart he exposed
himself to fatigues and performed feats of endurance
which a sound man might well have shirked. He
worked furiously and unceasingly. He kept his
balance and his courage under staggering blows of
ill-fortune. Never was there so impossible an
ambition as that of this sickly youth in a provincial
town, who desired, without any help, without even
any decent opportunities for self-instruction, to
obtain a scientific appointment. Yet he overcame
these obstacles and his ambition was fulfilled. And

when this was taken from him, when nothing was left but a few painful months of life and his Journal, when it was infinite labour even to trace a few words on the page, he continued the self-portrait which had become his last ambition, as long as he could hold a pen at all. The straggling, irregularly-formed letters which sprawl across the paper are the last witnesses of his invincible courage.

And to others this timid and cowardly young man seemed strong, masterful, difficult to manage, frightening, sometimes savage and bitter in conversation, but always magnetic and fascinating. " I know," he says, " I am not prepossessing in appearance—my nose is crooked and my skin is blotched." In reality his height, his distinction of bearing and fine hair produced an immediate effect of good looks—which, with the emaciation of his final days, changed into an austere and painful beauty. He had particularly beautiful hands, and his photographs certainly represent him as being not only noticeable but also attractive. The disparity between what he says of himself and what others thought of him involves no real contradiction. He is writing of the hidden and secret personality which no one else knew, and the fact that no one else could know this personality, save by his own deliberate act of revelation, is another proof of his strength. He is describing the other side of the moon.

His ambition was the one part of his secret life which was too great and too violent for even him to hide altogether. He might doubt his own qualities, but he could not conceal from himself or from others what he desired to be and to do. His ambitions were, he thought, very soon and very easily defeated, but the title he gave to his book, a catchpenny title, as he owned, and a little wanting in sincerity, confessed to a graver defeat than he actually sustained. His achievements were not great in bulk. His scientific triumph was the triumph of reaching a self-proposed aim in spite of almost impossible obstacles; but it was worth less in itself than as a witness to character. He might have become one of the greatest of English biologists; but promise is only promise, and this, besides, is promise of a kind with which we are not concerned here. " In time," he once said, " I should have revolutionised the study of Systematic Zoology." But he was not allowed time, and his scientific observations will be amplified, superseded, heaped under at last by an accumulation of the work of his successors. In literature his position is different.

When his book was being prepared for publi-cation, and while he was still ignorant what reception it would have, he remarked without hesitation that he " liked to look at himself posthumously as a writer "; and it appears from the introduction to *Enjoying Life* that his friends had long before expected him to turn his whole attention to litera-ture. Even here his work is comprised in small space. It consists of three things: the *Journal of a Disappointed Man*, containing extracts from his diaries between 1903 and 1917, the volume called *Enjoying Life and Other Literary Remains*, containing, together with a number of essays and articles, long passages omitted for the sake of space from the previous book, and the *Last Diary* which runs from the beginning of 1918 onwards. Even from these three small books certain deductions must be made. The scientific articles in the second volume were only just worth reprinting; and the essays on journal-writers and the two short stories, though they are promising, are yet no more than the experiments of a man who was thinking of giving himself formally to the profession of literature. But when all deductions are made, there is a residue which is considerable in value.

In the introduction to the first volume Mr. Wells very comprehensively lays stress on the circumstances of Barbellion's fate. He represents the diarist as saying, " You shall have at least one specimen carefully displayed and labelled. Here is a recorded unhappiness. When you talk about life and the rewards of life and the justice of life and its penalties, what you say must square with this." This is, of course, an aspect of the matter which no reader could manage to overlook, even if he desired (as he might conceivably desire) to do so. It would be a pity, however, if we were to consider it to the exclusion of every other aspect. Barbellion was not essentially a *specimen* who by good luck had the ability to display and label himself. If his circumstances had been quite other than they were, he would still have been a remarkable man and would almost certainly have done remarkable work. His disease and death ought to play the same part in our conception of him that they do in our conception of Keats, with whom, besides, he had certain affinities which he half-consciously recognised. We do not know what part disease played in creating or forcing or conditioning Keats's genius ; we only know that it infuses a poignancy and a colour into our picture of his life. He does not appear to us as the diseased poet, but as a poet who, as it happened, was stricken with disease. So with Barbellion: he had a personality and a gift for describing his experiences;

34

and, since it fell out that his experiences were tragic, therefore the story he tells is a tragedy. But the tragedy is not interesting only as such. It is interesting because the principal figure in it is Barbellion.

The comparison with Keats is natural, is suggestive, and can be supported by a number of particulars, both accidental and essential. " Since the fateful November 27th," says Barbellion, " my life has become entirely posthumous. I live now in the grave and am busy furnishing it with posthumous joys." Keats writes in his last letter, from Rome, " I have an habitual feeling of my real life having passed, and that I am leading a posthumous existence." But there is a closer similarity between them than the superficial parallel suggested by their use of the same image. Barbellion himself made the comparison more than once, and once in a very significant context.

" You can search all history " (he exclaims), " for an ambition more powerful than mine and not find it. No, not Napoleon, nor Wilhelm II., nor Keats."

And this uncontrollable ambition in both of them was one manifestation of the innermost ruling characteristic which they had in common, the passion for life in all its shapes and forms, for all the sensations life can bring, which inspires Barbellion's Journal as surely as it inspires Keats's poetry and letters.

The title of Barbellion's second book was not, as it might seem, intended in irony. He enjoyed life to a terrifying degree and could abandon himself to the ecstasy which it produced in him.

" As you say " (he writes in a letter, referring to a review of the Journal), " the rest of the notice distinguishing Marie Bashkirtseff from me by her zest for life is an astonishing and ludicrous misreading. Why, even since I became bedridden, as you will see some day, my zest for life took a devil of a lot of killing—like a sectioned worm with all the parts still wriggling. . . ."

In the last part of the diary his assertion is amply proved. Here the zest for life, in a man who could no longer indulge it save in memory, is sublimated to a piercing but sweet lyrical cry, which is one of the most moving utterances in recent literature. Before, when he was in possession of all his faculties, when the shadow of illness could sometimes be forgotten, it is a rapturous and boisterous expression of infinite energy, high spirits and gusto. Almost any paragraph in the essay called *Enjoying Life* would serve to demonstrate this:—

" ' *Dans littérature*,' said M. Taine, ' *j'aime tout*.' I would shake his hand for saying that and add: ' In life, Monsieur, as well.' All things attract me equally. I cannot concentrate. I am ready to do anything, go anywhere, think anything, read anything. Wherever I hitch my wagon I am confident of an adventurous ride. Somebody says, ' Come and hear some Wagner.' I am ready to go. Another, ' I say, they are going to ring the bull '—and who wants to complete his masterpiece or count his money when they are going to ring the bull ? I will go with you to Norway, Switzerland, Jericho, Timbuctoo. Talk to me about the Rosicrucians or the stomach of a flea and I will listen to you. Tell me that the Chelsea Power Station is as beautiful

36

as the Parthenon at Athens and I'll believe you. Everything is beautiful, even the ugly—why did Whistler paint the squalor of the London streets, or Brangwyn the gloom of a steam-crane? To subscribe to any one particular profession, mode of life, doctrine, philosophy, opinion or enthusiasm, is to cut oneself off from all the rest—I subscribe to all. With the whole world before you, beware lest the machinery of education seizes hold of the equipotential of your youth and grinds you out the finished product! You were a human being to start with—*now*, you are only a soldier, sailor, tinker, tailor. Leonardo da Vinci, racked with frustrate passion after the universal, is reported to have declared that only to do one thing and only to know one thing was a disgrace, no less."

Crying for the Moon, the essay which follows, also extracted from the Journal, is the obverse of the same coin:—

"I am passing through the world swiftly and have only time to live my own life. I am cut off by my own limitations and environment from knowing much or understanding much. I know nothing of literature and the drama; I have but little ear for music. I do not understand art. All these things are closed to me. I am passing swiftly along the course of my life with many others whom I shall never meet. How many dear friends and kindred spirits remain undiscovered among that number? There is no time for anything. Everything and every one is swept along in the hustling current. Oh! to sun ourselves awhile in the water meadows before dropping over the falls! The real tragedies in this world are not the things

37

which happen to us, but the things which don't happen."

There are critics who would trace the source of such outbursts as these and of the joy in life that constantly appears in Keats to the effects of bacterial disease. We cannot contradict the conclusion, which may have a certain truth. We can only point out that the same cause does not always produce the same effect, and we must therefore deduce a particular genius in those in whom this spirit manifests itself. Barbellion was, from one point of view, a case for pathology, but he was not, any more than was Keats, nothing but that. He had a fine temperament which he expressed very finely.

There is a temptation when one is considering the Journal, to which Barbellion's work must eventually be reduced, to consider it as so much raw material and to speculate how, if he had lived, he would have used the many talents he displays in it. He began it as a record of a naturalist's observations, and it developed only very gradually into a self-portrait and a repository for all his reflections and impressions. He was still, when his last illness overtook him, a professional scientist, scribbling in his diary at night for a hobby. But he was thinking of going over to literature; and one cannot help asking whether, if he had done so, he would not have turned his genius to some more formal and less miscellaneous method of expression. It is easy to discern in him any number of capacities. He might have become a critic—a statement which can be proved by a few examples taken at random:—

" I thoroughly enjoy Hardy's poetry for its

masterfulness, for his sheer muscular compulsion over the words and sentences. In his rough-hewn lines he yokes the recalcitrant words together and drives them along mercilessly with something that looks like simple, brute strength. . . . All this pleases me more, for I know to my cost what stubborn, sullen, hephæstian beasts, words and clauses can sometimes be. It is nice to see them punished. Hardy's poetry is Michael Angelo rather than Greek, Browning not Tennyson.

" It amuses me to discover the evident relish with which the author of *The Daffodil Fields* emphasises the blood and the flowers in the attack on Achi Baba. It's all blood and beautiful flowers mixed up together to Masefield's great excitement. . . . Still, to call Gallipoli ' bloody hell ' is, after all, only a pedantically exact description. You understand, tho', a very remarkable book—a work of genius.

". . . James Joyce's *Portrait of the Artist*—one of those books which the mob will take fifty years to discover but once discovered will again neglect."

He might have been a psychological or a satirical novelist, a metaphysician, a casual essayist. He might have been a poet of nature. His diaries are studded with exquisite descriptions of landscapes and living things, which grow only more vivid and moving as the end approaches and they become transcripts from memory instead of recent impressions. The last long entry in the Journal is one of them, and it is so good and so characteristic that it must be quoted here:—

" Rupert Brooke said the brightest thing in the world was a leaf with the sun shining on it.

God pity his ignorance! The brightest thing in the world is a Ctenophor in a glass jar standing in the sun. This is a bit of a secret, for no one knows about it save only the naturalist. I had a new sponge the other day and it smelt of the sea till I had soaked it. But what a vista that smell opened up !—rock pools, gobies, Blennies, anemones (crassicon, dahlia —oh! I forget). And at the end of my little excursion into memory I came upon the morning when I put some sanded opaque bits of jelly, lying on the rim of the sea, into a glass collecting jar and to my amazement and delight they turned into Ctenophors—alive, swimming, and iridescent! You must imagine a tiny soap-bubble about the size of a filbert with four series of plates or combs arranged regularly on the soap-bubble, from its North to its South Pole, and flashing spasmodically in unison as they beat on the water."

But I think that this way of looking on Barbellion's work, excusable as it might be, would nevertheless be mistaken. Every author writes the book that it is given to him to write, and Barbellion's book was the Journal. If, as seems very likely, he had developed altogether into a writer, he might still not have abandoned this form which had become by a gradual process peculiarly his own.

And this view is supported by the fact that up to the very last he was improving the flexible and accommodating method of literary expression which his diary had become. Towards the end it is obviously growing into something more than a diary: it is changing its character, turning into something which is subtly different in kind from the work of the diarists, his predecessors, with whom he has most often been compared. It does, without question, lose something by the change. It becomes less spontaneous, more suspect from the evidential point of view. But what it loses in the unconscious, it gains in the conscious.

The last eighteen months of it seem to me to show an advance on the third part of the published Journal almost as striking as the advance of that third part on the first. The form fitted very closely to Barbellion's many-sided and individual temperament; and, as time went on and he understood better what he was doing, he made it fit more closely still. It was a frame into which he could put with perfect ease all that his roving perceptions picked up in life: an impression of a landscape or an animal, a conversation overheard in the street, a suddenly flashing truth about himself or some other person, a general reflection upon humanity. As a journal-writer he is not, of course, alone; but being a strongly-marked personality, he is unique even among journal-writers. His intense interest in his own consciousness does not, as it did with Amiel, blind him to the actual outside world; he has more humour, more gusto in concrete detail than Marie Bashkirtseff, a vein of poetry that we do not find in Pepys. This is not intended to rank him above the writers with whom he loved to compare himself, but rather to emphasise his individuality among them.

We find ourselves at last wondering not how he would have employed the gifts he displays in the Journal, but to what pitch of excellence he would have brought the Journal itself. The last entries are admirably full of matter and admirably worded. The passage I have quoted on the Ctenophors is of great lyrical beauty—not a random jotting, but an impression seized and made permanent with something of the proportion and balance of a sonnet by Heredia. Over against it there might be quoted passages on the old village nurse who attended him for months, closely and humorously observed and set down without the waste of a syllable. Or there are pages of reflections like this:—

The Icons

" Every man has his own icon.

" Secreted in the closet of each man's breast is his icon, the image of himself, concealed from view with elaborate care, treated invariably with great respect, by means of which the Ego, being self-conscious, sees itself in relation to the rest of mankind, measures itself therewith, and in accordance with which it acts and moves and subsists. In the self-righteous man's bosom, it is a molten image of a little potentate who can do no wrong. In the egotist's, an ideal loved and worshipped by almost all men, addressed with solemnity and reverence, and cast in an immutable brazen form. Only the truth-seeker preserves his image in clay, covered in damp rags—a working hypothesis.

" A man towards his icon is like the tenderness and secretiveness of a little bird towards its nest, which does not know you have discovered its heart's treasure. For every one knows the lineaments of your image and talks about them to everybody else save you, and no one dare refer to his own—it is bad form—so that in spite of the gossip and criticism that swirls around each one's personality, a man remains sound-tight and insulated.

" The human comedy begins at the thought of the ludicrous unlikeness in many cases of the

42

treasured image to the real person—as much
verisimilitude about it as, say, about a bust by
Gaudier-Brzeska.

"Heavens! what a toy-shop it will be at the
Last Day! When all our little effigies are taken
from their cupboards, undraped, and ranged along
beside us, nude and shivering. In that Day
how few will be able to say that they ever
cried,—

"'God be merciful to me a sinner,' or 'a fool,'
or 'a humbug.'

"The human tragedy begins as soon as one
feels how often a man's life is ruined by simple
reason of this disparity between the image and
the real—the image (or the man's mistaken idea of
himself)—like an *ignis fatuus* leading him through
devious paths into the morass of failure, or worse
—of sheer, laughing-stock silliness. The moral
is:—

γνωθι σεαυτον

"(My dear chap, quoting Greek at your time of
life.)"

The mellowness and sweetness of these lines are
worth noting as characteristic of a transformation
which is obviously taking place through all the last
pages of the diary. This transformation adds
something in the nature of a rounding and a com-
pletion to the whole work which might otherwise
have been merely an interrupted record. It enlarges
too our conception of the author's character and
capacities and fills in, most graciously, our picture
of him.

Barbellion was accustomed to accuse himself of
being an egotist; but, on his own definition, he
was a truth-seeker. His portrait of himself was not

immutable. It grew clearer as he understood himself better and it changed as he changed. It was not complete when he died because his own development was not complete. But he carried it as far as he could and made of it a singular picture. His Journal is a book of an enduring sort, not merely because it is an accurate and candid self-portrait, but also because of the inherent attractions of its subject. Barbellion was a poet, a humourist, an observer, a philosopher, as well as a truthful, passionate and amazingly courageous man. In drawing a picture of the last he also made a picture of the world as it seemed to the first four, and thus captured in it poetry, humour, observation, and philosophy. The subject is still too fresh, and, by the vividness of its presentment, too painful, for any attempt at a final valuation to be made. Not long ago, Barbellion was still alive, suffering and hoping; and, with the best will in the world, no critic can avoid being influenced by this fact. But his book is a fair topic for prophecy; and it is not very rash to predict that, as it loses the sharpness and painfulness of a record of fact, so its qualities as a work of literature will come more into prominence and we shall realise that Barbellion was not only a genius untimely overwhelmed by an evil fate, but a genius who, before he was overwhelmed, had opportunity to do some at least of his appointed work. Then, whatever may be the theoretical views we hold on the connection between disease and genius, we shall be able to think less of Barbellion as a " case " and more of him as a writer. We shall not, perhaps, think that we have a complete portrait of him in his Journal any more than that we have a complete portrait of Keats in the *Odes* or even in the *Letters*. The greatest of artists cannot entirely disclose himself in his work. Barbellion did so no more than others. But he was an artist, and, between what he wrote of himself and what was otherwise revealed, it is possible to form a picture of a remarkable personality.

POSTSCRIPT

Professor A. F. Pollard, in an article which appeared in *History* after I had revised this essay for publication in book-form, seeks, under the form of a study in historical method, to dispute the genuineness of Barbellion's diaries. His specific arguments have been dealt with in a letter to *History* by Barbellion's brother, Mr. A. J. Cummings; and I will not go over them again here. I allude to the matter only because Professor Pollard suspects that three " literary artists " had a hand in the diaries. He seems to think that Mr. H. G. Wells was one of them ; and I suspect him of thinking that I was another. I certainly was not; and I am convinced that Professor Pollard is altogether deluding himself when he thinks that the diaries have been tampered with, otherwise than by their author.

The Life of Goethe

GOETHE lived on into his eighty-third year; and
Felix Mendelssohn, who saw him in his old age,
said that the world would come to believe that
there had been, not one, but many Goethes. This
has proved, in a literal sense, to be only too true.
During his long life he changed his mind many
times, held many contradictory opinions, assumed
many characters. The critic who wished to
describe the outcome of his experience as expressed
in his reflections on it would be hard put to it
to know what period to choose; and there is no
particular reason why the opinions of his seventieth
year should be thought more valid than those of
his fortieth. Yet every phase of his career is so
voluminously recorded that it seems to offer the
portrait of an independent being. Some writers
see him as a youthful lover to the exclusion of that
other phase in which he was an elderly flirt. To
some he is essentially a morbid and violent romantic,
to some a formalising classicist; to some a rationalist
and to some a mystic; to some the best of good
companions, to some a cold egotist; to some the
freest, most flexible spirit the German race has
ever produced; to some the typically pompous
and buttoned-up Geheimrat of legend. There is
justification for insisting on each of these impressions;
but their multitude makes synthesis difficult, and
of all possible syntheses perhaps the most misleading would be the easy conclusion that he was
" myriad-minded."

The difficulty is reflected accurately enough in
the vast literature which treats of Goethe and in

46

our natural attitude towards it. It is nearly ninety years since his death, and innumerable biographies of him exist; but we still hope that one which will be satisfactory may be produced. The posthumous work of Professor Hume Brown,[1] scholarly and laborious as it is, does not satisfy us. It is full, as full as Bielschowsky, without his preposterous inflations, without indeed the customary German reverence for the most frivolous or the most foolish utterance that issued from Goethe's mouth. It is, of course, more accurate than Lewes. But Lewes, who wrote so soon after Goethe's death, who never saw what German scholars call the *Urfaust*, who went astray, for want of sufficient information, over the complicated occasions of *Werther*—Lewes, has nevertheless written what is probably the best biography of Goethe in any language. He was not a poet, let alone a poet of Goethe's rank, but, to use an expressive phrase, he had " been there himself." His free intelligence, his wide range of interests, enabled him to distinguish, and to sympathise with, what was free and vital in Goethe's own work and character. He took Goethe's productions and the facts of his life at their intrinsic merits and made out of them a portrait which is reverent but not idolatrous.

It would not be quite true, of course, to say that all the other biographers of Goethe think their hero incapable of a fault. Professor Hume Brown admits that he was weak in will and quotes Emerson's judgment that he was not fundamentally an artist. But he cannot help writing of these things in such an odd way, which is not merely his own, as to give them insensibly the appearance of merits. Goethe was weak-willed; he was inartistic: perhaps,

[1] *Life of Goethe*. By P. Hume Brown. (Murray.)

in some mysterious manner which we are unable to understand, these qualities are of the essence of true greatness! The parody, of course, if it were applied to Professor Hume Brown, would be extremely unfair; it would take the most abysmal of German commentators to express so fatuous a thought. But such are the feelings, whatever element of caricature they may contain, with which we rise from these two volumes, as from so many of their predecessors. The traditional image of Goethe issues from these pages, a little flawed perhaps but substantially unbroken, an Olympian who embraced in one mind and one life all the knowledge, all the interests, all the experience possible to humanity. But it would probably be more accurate to say that the contradictions of Goethe's personality mean, not so much that he reconciled in himself many tendencies usually incompatible, as that obscure elements in his character, assisted by misfortunes of circumstance, hindered him in doing things which he wished to do and which, at first sight, his endowments would seem to have made possible for him. He was truly a marvellous man, but in many ways tragically marvellous. There is perhaps no case in literature in which gifts so great have been so often frustrated by apparently trifling but really insuperable difficulties.

Goethe, it has been said, has compensated mankind for the almost total loss of the biography of Shakespeare. Here, at least, we have the life of a genius set out on the heroic scale and with encyclopedic minuteness. He is esteemed the greatest poet of a people which holds art and learning in high respect and has a traditional devotion to scholarly research; and he himself deliberately

laid the foundations on which succeeding generations of students have reared an impressive edifice.
Many eyewitnesses have left their impressions of
him; his correspondence has been preserved in
almost unequalled profusion; he devoted a long
book to a record, more careful than candid, to be
sure, of his first twenty-six years. More than
this, little that he wrote is, by his own confession,
without its corresponding and illuminating fragment
of biographical knowledge.

His life naturally attracts both biographer and
reader by its variety, its richness of incident and the
fact that hardly any part of it is mere dumb detail,
uninterpreted by the poet himself, speaking as
poet. He was the son of a well-to-do citizen of
Frankfort, a precocious child and a still more precocious youth; and when he entered upon the first
excitements of manhood he noted and illustrated
their effects on him in an abundant series of fresh
and beautiful lyrics. His appearance—though his
good looks as a youth have probably been exaggerated—attracted all who met him and commonly
sent them off to their notebooks to record their
impressions. He startled Europe with *Werther*;
invented, or at any rate popularised, a new kind
of folly; caused no one knows how many suicides;
and influenced the dress of a continent. Wertherism
was then as great a force as Byronism later—it was
indeed one of the direct sources of Byronism—and
Chinese painters took scenes from the book for
subjects. This wave of fame floated him into the
ducal court at Weimar, where, to the astonishment
of all, he developed from a boon-companion of
the young Duke into a hard-working and capable
Minister of State. He held this position for ten
years, thereby proving himself superior to the

charges usually preferred against poets of vagueness and impracticability, and ended it by that dramatic departure for Italy which divides his career in two and seems to typify the longing of all poets for the south. He formed with Schiller the most impressive of all literary friendships. He met Napoleon, and extorted his admiration—" *Voilà un homme !* " said Napoleon, as the poet entered the room. In his old age he was one of the wonders of Europe—a goal of pilgrimages. He was even so fortunate as to utter in his last delirium words capable of bearing an allegorical interpretation.

His numerous love-affairs, in particular, charm biographers and throw an especial glow of poetry over what might be otherwise too serious a story. Scholars no longer young, whom one would have supposed to have outgrown such interests, learnedly debate whether this young lady or that is properly to be included in the canon. It begins, perhaps, in the most catholic versions, with Gretchen, of whom we know nothing more, not even her surname, but that she led the boy into bad company and did not return his affection. Kätchen Schönkopf, at Leipzig, fails to qualify thoroughly by reason of her failure to inspire any poem of the first order. Friederike Brion, the pastor's daughter of Sesenheim, was the occasion of the first great affair, which, to be sure, we know almost solely from Goethe's own, certainly inaccurate, account. He abandoned himself entirely to this passion for several months, and while it lasted he wrote *Wilkommen und Abschied, Ich komme bald, ihr goldnen Kinder,* and a dozen other pieces which make as fine and tender an expression of young love, the first physical intoxication of sense and spirit, as it has ever received. After a time he remembered himself, extricated himself, and brusquely departed, to do penance for the betrayal by scourging the treachery of Weislingen, of Clavigo, and of Faust.

There follows the affair with Lotte Buff, when he was saved from too deep an engagement by Lotte's previous betrothal, and the affair with Maximiliane Brentano, when he was not saved from burning his fingers, from scenes and humiliations, by the lady's marriage. He telescoped the two affairs, and out of them he made *Werther*. Then came Lili Schönemann and the loves of the citizen's son and the young lady of fashion, which resulted in a disconcertingly unexpected betrothal. The poems he wrote on this subject are, in a different manner, as beautiful as those inspired by Friederike; and they are, for reasons to which I shall return, psychologically much more interesting. Again he extricated himself, went to Weimar, and began the long connection with Charlotte von Stein, which is commemorated in *Iphigenie auf Tauris* and *Tasso*. On his return from Italy he quarrelled with her and took under his protection a young woman who had been employed in an artificial-flower factory, Christiane Vulpius. She is the subject of the sensual, richly-decorated *Römische Elegien* and of a few other poems of the same kind. In 1806, when the liaison had lasted twenty years, he married her. There remains Minna Herzlieb, the heroine of the sonnets; Marianne von Willemer, the heroine (and part-author) of the *West-östlicher Divan*; and Ulrike von Levetzow, the heroine of the *Trilogie der Leidenschaft*, to whom, when she was seventeen and he seventy-two, he sent an offer of marriage

51

by the hand of the Grand Duke Karl August himself.

The catalogue of Goethe's loves involves a catalogue of a good deal of the best poetry he ever wrote. But there is more to be considered, and, besides, the character of the whole must be considered. He was, of course, unfortunate in his country and his age. Germany, still recovering from the Thirty Years' War, was centuries behind the other great nations of the West in the production of a literature. Between Walther von der Vogelweide and Goethe there is hardly any figure to be seen in pure literature save the rather sugary poets of the Breslau school, the true but small talent of Claudius, and the slightly unsympathetic talent of Lessing. Goethe was born into the flattest of landscapes, with no elders whom he could respect and no contemporaries to rival him. It was not until the maturity of Schiller that Germany could provide any man even approaching his equal. He was therefore without models, standards, or guides, a genius working in the void, with nothing done for him and all to do. He became early conscious of the emptiness of German literature and looked outside its boundaries for assistance. There he found a whole world of forms created and established by generations of artists—the forms of Homer, Shakespeare, Racine, Molière, Sophocles, Propertius, Petrarch. He set feverishly to work to import these into his own country, to make himself the great creator of genres in German literature. As a result, in spite of the range and variety of his work, in spite of his genius and original mind, he failed in, or rather never attempted, that fundamental duty of a great poet, the creation of a form suited to himself. For *Faust*, though it is not copied or imported, is not a form, not a logical and harmonious growth from a central inspiration, but a convenient receptacle for a number of ideas and passages of different sorts on wholly different levels of value and intensity.

This misfortune does indeed injure to a considerable extent the artistic value of his total work, of which there is only one section quite exempt from its influence. The greater number of his lyrical poems was based on, and developed from, native models, from the traditional songs which Herder at Strassburg first taught him to find, to study, and to enjoy. Here something was done for him, something was ready at hand which he could transmute to his own uses by a genuine exercise of the formative faculty instead of by the more mechanical work of transplantation from the Greek or the English into the German language. Of all his work, Goethe's songs and ballads make the part which we feel to be most truly, indefeasibly, his own. They spring out of the traditional poetry, but not by the way of imitation. Goethe was not concerned, as are always the makers of sham ballads, to copy, perhaps more carefully than anything else, the accidental quaintnesses and naïveties which at first sight seem to be their most characteristic peculiarities. He went behind their surface appearances and drew on as much of the spirit and modes of thought, which first made them, as could serve him for his own purposes of personal expression.

But songs and ballads of love and country life and simple emotions, however excellent they may be, will not make a great poet of the rank commonly granted to Goethe, nor will they altogether account for the genius which we believe him to have possessed. We must turn to his other works, his more ambitious works, if we are to find the counterpart of Homer and Virgil, of Dante and Shakespeare. When we do so, what a disappointment it is! What treasures of wisdom and poetry we find in these great compositions, and yet how poor seems the whole by the side of the achievements with which it has been compared. Yet our feeling that the comparison can, and should, be made is not wholly effaced. Goethe is, in fact, a poet who is equal to this rank by his natural endowments but not by his actual performance. Professor Hume Brown remarks with justice how great a part of his work is made up of fragments and unfinished failures. A long succession of these runs from the great *Prometheus* and *Der Ewige Jude* of early years to the *Aufgeregten*, the *Nausikaa*, *Achilleis* and *Natürliche Tochter* of the second half of his life. It is almost a miracle that *Faust* should have been rescued, after many years, from this fate; and its rescue was accomplished only on the condition that it should lose its unity and consistency. Of the other fragments, either of the two first-named might very well have become what Goethe never did produce, a complete and self-sufficing poem cast in a form necessary and peculiar to its author and to itself. *Prometheus* was to have been a dithyrambic drama, written in an extremely vigorous and flexible kind of free verse, a drama drawing modern significance from an ancient myth. But it was doomed not to be even half finished. *Der Ewige Jude*, which was hardly more than begun, would have been an even more remarkable production. Goethe intended in it a long, comprehensive, half-satirical, half-philosophical narrative of the development of the Christian world; and

54

the fragment he did write has astonishing power, together with a freedom and penetration of wit which seem to anticipate Heine.

Even in *Faust*, the best part, from the strictly poetic point of view, is the central fragment which Goethe wrote before he went to Weimar. The rest, splendid as it sometimes is, was taken up by an older, less enthusiastic man and carried out in a different manner. It formally completes the fragment, tells the whole story connectedly, and gives the tragedy a more or less symmetrical shape. But the amplification, even apart from the quite irrelevant *Intermezzo*, is largely an attempt to give it a philosophical meaning which is not always raised into poetry. Goethe was inspired, as a young man, by the characters of Faust and Mephistopheles— by a Mephistopheles as concrete, as fully embodied, as that of Marlowe or the Satan of *Paradise Lost* —and in these early scenes the wider significance of their pact and its fulfilment was implicit in what they had to say, was indeed *poetically* apprehended by the author—for it is one of the functions of poetry to particularise, and thoroughly to particularise, general ideas. But later on Goethe resolved that these characters should express an attitude towards the world which had become anterior in his mind to his conception of themselves. *Faust* may be, perhaps, the greatest of modern poems; but its deficiencies become terribly obvious when we compare it with the *Divine Comedy* (which Goethe despised) or the tragedies of Shakespeare.

When we examine his other completed works we see at once how much he suffered from the temptation to import his forms readymade from other literatures. In *Götz von Berlichingen* he did most patently what he avoided when he drew inspiration from the traditional songs of his own country: he copied the errors, the accidental characteristics of the Shakespearean drama, at least as carefully as any other part of it. This was perhaps a fault of the undiscriminating enthusiasm of youth. Look, then, at the famous *Hermann und Dorothea*, the work of his forty-eighth year. For this country idyll he adopted deliberately as close an approximation as he could manage to the manner of Homer.

" Und es sagte darauf der edle, verständige
        Pfarrherr,
    Er, die Zierde der Stadt. . . .

" Sorgsam brachte die Mutter des klaren herr-
        lichen Weines,
    In geschliffener Flasche auf blankem zinner-
        nem Runde,
    Mit den grünlichen Römern, den echten
        Bechern des Rheinweins."[1]

It is indeed astonishing how well Goethe adapts the characteristics of his original to his own purpose: it is a never-failing miracle of dexterity. But are not these such exclamations as we use for the fit of borrowed garments? Should we be so much impressed by the way in which they fit here and there if there were not other places in which they do not fit at all? One can perhaps imagine Goethe, if he had received any support from his own

---

[1] " And thereon spoke the noble, judicious parson, he, the ornament of the town."

" Carefully the mother brought them of the clear lordly wine, in a polished flagon on the shining tin tray, with the green glasses, the right beakers for Rhine wine."

language, working out for this poem a style which might have been, as it were, the equivalent of that which Wordsworth worked out for somewhat similar purposes. But he had no such support: he was condemned to adaptations. Of these probably the most successful is to be found in the *Römische Elegien*, where he used the elegiac couplets of what he called " Amor's Triumvirs," Ovid, Tibullus, and Propertius, to describe his passion for Christiane. But was it not here that in the first place he borrowed from the poets the precise cast of feeling which afterwards he expressed in a style also borrowed from them ?

As we go further we find faults of other sorts. *Werther* is perhaps artistically the most equal of all Goethe's productions. The flow and stream of its splendid prose, the most lucid written in German before the appearance of Heine and still the most eloquent, preserves the reader's interest alive until the end, but the spirit of the book suffers a degeneration which was sufficiently indicated by Goethe when he remarked that while the hero is sane he reads Homer, but Ossian when he is beginning to go mad. It degenerates, that is to say, not outwardly but inwardly, from the noble to the maudlin. *Wilhelm Meister* is richly heavy with wisdom; but how, we cannot help asking, could any novelist, writing so tolerantly of what Carlyle amiably called " players and libidinous actresses," write at the same time so dully, without giving his work even a scandalous attraction ? Among the plays, *Tasso* has the most continuous beauty of style and a radical defect of substance, a defect which, in Goethe, sprang from deep origins and is very symptomatic. This divinely serene conversation,

57

broken by only six physical movements of the characters, conceals, without denying, the tragedy of its hero. Tasso is here not a great poet who finds himself astray in the real world and ends in the madhouse, but merely a sensitive spirit goaded into an exaggerated display of feeling, an hysteria, from which he will in time recover. This is not a transmutation of the fact but a shrinking from it; and it was characteristic of Goethe that he did always shrink from any excessively painful fact. When he permitted a tragic ending, for once, to the first part of *Faust*, the second part had to begin with a scene in which, by flowers and soft breezes and the song of birds, the spirits restore Faust (not Gretchen, by the way) to calm and happiness.

This is, I own, a sufficiently cursory and incomplete catalogue, and one deliberately directed to the discovery of faults instead of the discovery of beauties. It would be possible to reverse the point of view and make a great reckoning on the other side. But no such reckoning, I think, could ever remove the strong sense of dissatisfaction remaining in the mind of any one who searches Goethe for large achievements worthy of a poet on the greatest scale. It is true—and this is perhaps the most interesting point—that any one who does so will find many things not unworthy of a very good poet, and many things, even, not unworthy of Goethe's reputation and gifts. But these things are rarely the same. There are good poetical things, there are examples of wisdom and insight; but where Goethe is most successful as a poet he is not often on the highest level of significance, and where his conception is widest, it is generally not quite fused into poetry.

" Grau, theurer Freund, ist alle Theorie
    Und grün des Lebens goldner Baum." [1]

How magical and stimulating are those lines when
we first discover them; what a shaft of light they
throw down into Faust's library! But they are
only the expression of a mood, a statement which is
partial, not comprehensive.

" Es bildet ein Talent sich in der Stille,
    Sich ein Charakter in dem Strom der Welt." [2]

—that is wise and valuable, but versification, which
has made it tersely epigrammatic, has not made it
poetry.

If the distinction is clear and the argument
recommends itself, then the conclusion is easy
enough and perhaps sufficient. But the disparity
between Goethe's gifts and what he accomplished
must spring from some element in his character,
and it is interesting to inquire what this may have
been, all the more because his position is not
merely that of a great poet, but also of a great and
exemplary figure. This element might be sought
by several different channels of approach, but there
is one which has been already mentioned and is
the easiest.

Lewes's remarks on the affair with Friederike
are distinguished throughout by his usual strong
common sense—never more so than when he dis-
poses of the notion that Goethe jilted her in order
to " remain true to his genius." " Had he loved

[1] " Gray, dear friend, is theory, and green the golden tree of
life."

[2] " Talent is formed in quietude, but character in the flow of
the world."

her enough to share a life with her," says Lewes, " his experience of women might have been less extensive, but it would assuredly have gained an element it wanted. It would have been deepened. . . . The kiss he feared to press upon the loving lips of Friederike—the life of sympathy he refused to share with her—are wanting to the greatness of his works." This really expresses the truth in a way that need only amplification and illustration, though Lewes for some reason lost sight of it and did not pursue it further. It contains a truth which is valid to some extent in almost all the relations of Goethe's life.

He frequently spoke of himself—and his admirers, contemporary and later, have accepted his testimony—as being possessed by a dæmon, as having in his nature an incalculable force which, were it not wisely bridled, might carry him helplessly to ruin. Perhaps his fear of this force and the limits he set upon it were greater realities in his life than it was itself. We see him generally possessed by caution and prudence, a man for ever drawing back. It is certain that he never rushed into disaster : it is not certain that he might not have been more fully, more satisfactorily, the poet he was intended to be if he had occasionally taken the risk of it. The influence of women was perhaps one of the greatest of the dangers that opened before him. He was unboundedly inflammable ; but he contrived—and " contrived " is the word —to remain single up to the age of fifty-seven. Men of dæmonic character are very frequently unhappy in their married lives; but I do not think that we see them very frequently enjoying quite so many hairbreadth escapes from that most serious of all human decisions. It is not as though Goethe's

60

affairs were commonly of the kind that does not lead up to marriage. They were, on the contrary, precisely of the kind that, in the ordinary way, entails marriage as a natural consequence: yet only once was he so much as betrothed. The occasion on which this happened is of considerable interest.

When Goethe, in writing *Dichtung und Wahrheit*, reached the episode of Lili Schönemann, he told Eckermann that his love for her had been the most powerful he had known in his life. Lewes rather oddly dismisses this as the forgetfulness of an old man (he has a strong partiality for Friederike and Christiane—so queerly do Goethe's amours affect his biographers!) but I think that both in *Dichtung und Wahrheit* and in the poems of the time good evidence can be found for putting the most literal interpretation on his statement. Lili is almost, if not absolutely, the most vivid figure in the autobiography. Friederike is little more than an element entering into the composition of a poetic scene, a decorative person, with not much to say for herself; but Lili is a vigorous, determined girl, whose personality is a factor in the events in which she takes part.

There was a disparity of position between Goethe and Lili as great as there had been in the case of Friederike, but now the aspiration was on his side, not on hers. He approached her with difficulty and unwillingly. He came of a sober, middle-class family ; she and her mother were ladies of fashion; their religions were different; and, what seemed conclusive to the elder Goethe, the Schönemanns were leading an expensive life on a doubtfully sufficient income. The position seemed hopeless ; but a third party, a woman, busied herself in the matter, removed the opposition of the two families, and triumphantly bade the lovers embrace. " I stood," says Goethe, " opposite to Lili and held out my hand to her. She, not delaying indeed, but still slowly, laid hers in it. After a deep breath, we fell, strongly moved, in one another's arms." The course of the affair was what this would suggest. Eventually Goethe created a breach by omitting fully to resume relations when he returned after an absence from Frankfort.

But the poems he wrote for Lili are even more eloquent than the material facts. They were couched from the first, though at first of course playfully, in the form of complaints.

> " Warum ziehst du mich unwiderstehlich,
>   Ach in jene Pracht ?
> War ich, guter Junge, nicht so selig
>   In der öden Nacht ? "[1]

But as time goes on the playfulness disappears. In *Lilis Park* he represents himself as the half-tamed, wholly mutinous bear, threatens that he will break away from her, boasts that he still has the strength. He made the attempt, travelled to Switzerland with a friend, reached a mountain-pass whence he could see below him the plains of Italy, and was forced by his longing to return.

> " Wie ein Vogel der den Faden bricht
>   Und zum Walde kehrt,
>   Er schleppt, des Gefängnisses Schmach,

[1] " Why do you draw me irresistibly into this splendour ? Was I not, good, simple young man that I am, happy in the empty night ? "

Noch ein Stückchen des Fadens nach:
Er ist der alte freigeborne Vögel night,
Er hat schon jemand angehört." [1]

There is in this a curious note of bitterness which
is not natural to Goethe: the exclamation of a man
who is afraid of something and resents it. It is
easier to understand it when one sees in *Dichtung
und Wahrheit* how deep was the impression which
Lili's strength of character made on him. There
he describes how once, when she was offended by
something a stranger said at table, " without
changing the sweetness of her expression, she
brushed her right hand quite prettily across the
tablecloth, and composedly pushed on to the floor
all that stood in the way of her gentle movement."
The incident is curious, the picture of it strikingly
real. Lili seems to have been in that circle a
person of equal importance with Goethe, with an
equal licence for self-expression. He speaks of
her, as he did not always of Friederike, as an equal
and sometimes with genuine humility. And she
frightened him more than any one else he ever
met in his life, because, more than any one else,
she threatened to invade his mental independence.

There are other traits in his character which
reinforce the impression produced by this episode.
Among these, one of the most noticeable is his
hatred of interview of farewell, which is perhaps
a special form of his reluctance to speak of any
project before it was actually carried out. Thus
he effected his breach with Friederike, in a somewhat cowardly manner, by letter after he had

[1] " Like a bird who breaks the thread which holds him and
returns to the wood, he drags after him, shameful sign of his
bondage, still a scrap of the thread. He is not the old, free-born
bird, he has been some one's property."

returned to Frankfort; he left Wetzlar in the midst of his perturbations there, leaving a note for Lotte and Albert, who had shared and suffered with him; he set out for Italy for a long sojourn, without warning any of his friends, even Frau von Stein, though it had been by no means a sudden decision. This was the initial, and, one would think, sufficient, cause of his quarrel with Frau von Stein, who resented his want of confidence in her.

But the thing was native in him, a trick constantly repeated. It sprang from his ruling desire to be his own master and from his knowledge that he could satisfy that desire only by following very special courses of behaviour. In his early years he called himself a chameleon. The truth of the charge is demonstrated by the ease with which he fell successively under different influences, now Behrisch, now Herder, now Merck, and by the way in which his youthful letters and professions accommodate themselves to the taste of his several correspondents. He was determined to make his own decisions, to be himself; but he knew that he was not strong enough to withstand the influence of his friends, if ever he should admit them too far into his life. The only safety for his mental independence lay in withdrawing himself.

This is the secret of that mask of ice-like inflexibility and self-sufficiency which the later Goethe assumed and which terrified all beholders. It covered an impressionable, feminine spirit, only too ready to obey the will of any person who could get at it. Goethe came at last to live alone because he could not share his life with any one and remain himself. Even with Schiller, during the whole course of that long and impressive connection, the note of reserve is more evident than the note of

64

intimacy. It is true that the freedom of their intellectual intercourse was complete; ideas flowed between them without check or hesitation, and the mind of each was fully opened to the other. But it was only his mind that Goethe opened to his friend. He showed towards him none of the irrational, affectionate, spontaneous impulses which prove that the inward springs of the spirit are loosened.

This element in Goethe's character governed the whole of his work, the whole of his thought. It limited his knowledge of life, and it restrained him, after his earliest years, from ever throwing himself into his work with that complete self-forget-fulness which is necessary if the last degree of excellence is to be obtained. He could not wholly forget himself in anything, save with peril to his painfully won, precariously maintained mental balance. He never underwent, in life or in art, that salutary experience of surrender to something stronger than himself—simply because whenever he encountered something stronger than himself he ran away from it. It is this which makes him so noticeably avoid the element of tragedy in his poetry, which turns the catastrophe of Tasso into no more than a painful breach of good manners. It is this instinctive shrinking from unpleasant and unmanageable fact which betrays him into his occasional turns of fatuity, as when he gives for his sole reflection on the profoundly disturbing affair of Lili the remark that " it was a strange decision of the high powers which dispose of us that, in the course of my wonderful existence, I should experience also what it feels like to be betrothed."

To a man capable of that thought we do not turn in our moments of deepest feeling either for counsel or for comfort. Goethe knew a great deal about life, but he preserved himself for eighty-three years from any too close experience of it. He is the observer seated on the water's edge whose keen sight penetrates very far down into the depths; but he is necessarily without the more poignant, if more restricted, knowledge of the man who has fallen in, who knows from immediate experience that water is wet and what it feels like to drown.

And yet, after all, when one has considered that mind and that work, how natural it is to turn back on oneself and exclaim, with Arnold, " My voice shall never be joined to those which decry Goethe." " Goethe's profound, imperturbable naturalism," says Arnold again, " is absolutely fatal to all routine thinking; he puts the standard once for all inside every man instead of outside him; when he is told such a thing must be so, there is immense authority and custom in favour of it being so, it has been held to be so for a thousand years, he answers with Olympian politeness, ' But *is* it so ? Is it so to *me* ? ' " And in truth the first business of criticism is to find out what things are, and what they are worth, rather than to complain because they are not something else. That I should so naturally say this is in itself evidence that Goethe has lived, evidence of years spent under his guidance. He did his work, he made his contribution to our thought, he has his place in the history of humanity, even if these things should be discovered not to be quite what they have been supposed. Perhaps one of the ways of seeing life steadily and seeing it whole is not to see it too close. If one keeps far enough away from it, its vibrations cannot impair the steadiness of the observation.

Goethe had a wide and shallow mind. His

knowledge of humanity is excelled in every particular aspect by some one; but only very rarely has so great a range of knowledge been held in a single mind. His disinclination to engage himself too firmly in anything assisted the constant shifting of his point of view, from romantic to classic, and back to romantic again, from Christian to pagan and back again to Christianity, so that in the end he had at least sampled almost every possible mode of thought. We do not go to him, as I have said, for help in distress, but we can go to him for as much as any detached observer can tell us of something we are about to experience. No one who has allowed himself to feel fully the influence of Goethe's mind will ever look at the world again in quite the same way. We have only to guard against the two extremes, one of which is regarding him as an all-adequate guide to life while the other lies in casting him aside as soon as he proves in any particular case not to be adequate.

The Poetry of Mr. Walter de la Mare [1]

THE poetry of Mr. de la Mare is fortunate in
being almost universally admired, equally by the
idolaters and by the enemies of tradition, by the
reading public at large as well as, in a very special
way, by the members of his own calling. And so
far it has not done what often, after a time, obscures
the beauty of an original style and brings it, if only
passingly, into disrepute: it has not yet raised up
a flock of too faithful imitators. It remains unique
and unvulgarised, the sole contemporary flower of
a strain in its predecessors, clearly novel, yet clearly
continuing a tradition in English poetry. The
forerunners of Mr. de la Mare are, chiefly, Coleridge
and Poe, and, beyond them and in a somewhat
different way, Christina Rossetti. His superficial,
and, I suspect, conscious resemblance to the third
of these is the greatest. Which of them wrote:—

" Come to me in the silence of the night;
    Come in the speaking silence of a dream " ?

And which wrote:—

" There came a pedlar to an evening house;
    Sweet Lettice, from her lattice looking down,
    Wondered what man he was, so curious
    His black hair dangled on his tattered gown " ?

Many of the poems in *Songs of Childhood*, Mr. de
la Mare's first book, have distinct affinities with
Goblin Market and *Maiden-Song*, and throughout

[1] *Poems,* 1901 *to* 1918. Two volumes. (Constable.)

68

his work of this sort Miss Rossetti's influence has often counted for something. But, generally speaking, he has not her peculiar power of tight, exact, sufficient writing, her hard, clear line, and she has not his peculiar power of suggesting the inexplicable. It is this power which he shares with Coleridge and Poe and which makes him their modern successor. We call it, unsatisfactorily but inevitably, " magic." In him, as in them, it expresses itself often enough through a fantastic or dreamlike character in the imagery and through almost unanalysable subtleties in the rhythm. I mention their names here not for the purpose of instituting comparisons or of tracing their influence on him (they have had indeed very little), but so as to indicate a quality which is more easily distinguished thus, than described.

Mr. de la Mare's earliest work was produced rather later than that of most poets, but there is less in it than is usual with others for him to be ashamed of, and it shows him already aware of, and understanding, the fundamental qualities of his own genius. The pieces in *Songs of Childhood* (1901) and *Poems* (1906) have not an average level so high as that of the later volumes, and there are in them a good many technical blemishes, from some of which it has evidently since cost the poet much time and trouble to free himself. He was occasionally given to clumsy and ugly inversions, from which one would have thought his love of Miss Rossetti would have freed him, and to the use of false and affected words. The atrocious adverb " wonderly " appeared as late as the *Motley* volume of 1918, but has now, in the collected edition, given way to " wondrously "—causing in the reader a slight surprise that Mr. de la Mare

did not think of that before. In *Poems* he was
capable of writing such a verse as this—gauche,
angular, and inexpressive:—

> " Thou canst not see; *I* see, dearest;
>   O, then, yet patient be,
> Though love refuse thy heart all rest,
> Though even love wax angry, lest
>   Love should lose *thee* ? "

In the same collection he placed a curious imitation
of Spenser's allegorical beasts, and a number of
sonnets, not all of which show genuine feeling for
the form or anything but the will to comply with
its mechanical necessities.

But in these two books there is plenty that no
one else could have written, and plenty that prophesied unmistakably (or so it seems now) his future
power. Among the *Songs of Childhood* there are
several pieces which could have gone into *Peacock
Pie*, published twelve years afterwards, without
causing the slightest feeling of incongruity. There
are also most characteristic pieces of a different
sort, such as *Alulvan* :—

> " The sun is clear of bird and cloud,
>   The grass shines windless, gray and still,
> In dusky ruin the owl dreams on,
>   The cuckoo echoes on the hill ;
> Yet soft along Alulvan's walks
>   The ghost at noonday stalks.
>   .   .   .   .
>
> All night the fretful, shrill Banshee
>   Lurks in the ivy's dark festoons,
> Calling for ever, o'er garden and river,
>   Through magpie changing of the moons:

' Alulvan, O, alas! Alulvan,
      The doom of lone Alulvan! ' "

This is crude enough compared with what Mr. de
la Mare has done since. The internal rhyme in
" Calling for ever, o'er garden and river," is out
of keeping with the rest of the rhythm; and the
Banshee is not a fortunate stroke of the imagination
—one cannot help seeing it swinging in the ivy
by its tail. But the poem, in its cadences and its
atmosphere, is the precursor of many in which
a similar inspiration is expressed with more sureness and cunning. " Alulvan " is never long
absent from Mr. de la Mare's verse, by whatever
name he calls it—Arabia, or " a dark château," or
" the courts of the Lord Pthamasar." In the same
volume there is a piece of sheer metrical beauty
which points forward to similar but finer achievements:—

> " There is a wind where the rose was;
>   Cold rain where sweet grass was;
>   And clouds like sheep
>   Stream o'er the steep
>   Gray skies where the lark was.
>
> Nought gold where your hair was;
> Nought warm where your hand was;
>   But phantom, forlorn,
>   Beneath the thorn,
>   Your ghost where your face was. . . ."

It required genuine inspiration to make so lovely
an effect out of material so uncompromisingly
sibilant.

First Essays on Literature

The earliest known and most popular part of Mr. de la Mare's work was, naturally, the poetry which he has written for children. Naturally—because any sort of literature which serves a definite and immediate purpose must get a start in time over that which does not. And these poems do serve a purpose: children do like them. There is not enough verse in the world, written for children, which children really enjoy and which intelligent parents can bear to see them enjoying, to hinder the recognition of Mr. de la Mare's great gift for this kind of writing. His two collections, *Songs of Childhood* and *Peacock Pie*, contain certain poems which might have gone just as well elsewhere, are not indeed strictly intended for children. (It is true that children frequently like these pieces as much as the others; but then they frequently like *Paradise Lost*, *The Grave*, and *The Dawn in Britain*—quite comprehensibly.) Both collections do, in fact, appeal to others besides children, offer a good deal more than most children can understand. They are both suffused with the general spirit of Mr. de la Mare's work, of which I shall speak more at length later. But they are valuable for their immediate purpose because they are full of bright, definite pictures and of fantastic things. Fairies, goblins, and witches, the dwarfs " Alliolyle, Lallerie, Muziomone " appeal to a child, and so do exact and vivid descriptions of the common things it knows. Thus on the one side in *Peacock Pie*, we have:—

" Clapping her platter stood plump Bess,
    And all across the green
  Came scampering in, on wing and claw,
    Chicken fat and lean :—

Dorking, Spaniard, Cochin China,
  Bantams sleek and small,
Like feathers blown in a great wind,
  They came at Bessie's call."

It takes a grown-up, no doubt, to understand
precisely how remarkable a piece of work that is,
to appreciate how exquisitely chosen are the strokes
of description that make up the picture, and how
great is the poet's tact in saying so much and no
more. But the child does what is really essential
when it enjoys the picture. Children can be devoted
realists: they have, more than their elders, that
faculty which Nietzsche required in his superman,
of accepting life so fully that they demand more
of it, all the same things over again in infinite
repetition. There is a great number of poems of
this sort—*Mima*, *The Dunce*, *Bread and Cherries*,
" *Sooeep !* " and many more, all ministering to the
same desire. On the other side we have the purely
joyous fantasy of:—

    " Ann, Ann!
      Come! quick as you can!
    There's a fish that *talks*
      In the frying-pan.
    Out of the fat,
      As clear as glass,
    He put up his mouth
      And moaned ' Alas! '
    Oh, most mournful,
      ' Alas, alack! '
    Then turned to his sizzling,
      And sank him back."

Mr. de la Mare knows, too, and can describe, the

small secret pleasures of childhood—the pleasure, for example, of staring from behind a curtained window at people in the street and reflecting that none of them knows he is watched; and the child loves to recognise itself in a book. He is even so much at home with his audience that he can venture on a little moral instruction: *Poor Henry* is an appeal to the young to take their physic without protest, but it is not offensive. *Peacock Pie* has been published, strangely enough, in an illustrated edition; but it is for children a picture-book in itself, where no competition ought to be risked with the images which the reader can derive so immediately from the poet's words. These images, whether it is fact or fancy that they embody, are sufficiently sharp and realistic. Note the one appeal to the eye in the poem last quoted, the fat " as clear as glass," and observe how vivid it is and how satisfying to a child who likes fantasy properly substantiated.

From this series of pictures the way of transition to Mr. de la Mare's other work is not hard to find, for his poetry throughout is rich in pictorial power. He has a region of his own which has already been exemplified in *Alulvan* and of which there will be more to say later; but he can also make most beautiful pictures of ordinary scenes and things. *The Scarecrow* is one example of this, *The Linnet* another, and *The Bells* another:—

> " Shadow and light both strove to be
> The eight bell-ringers' company,
> As with his gliding rope in hand,
> Counting his changes, each did stand;
> While rang and trembled every stone,
> To music by the bell-mouths blown:

Till the bright clouds that towered on high
Seemed to re-echo cry with cry."

The arts with which, here and elsewhere, he manages
to content the eye are of the slightest sort, but they
are sufficient. He has not the curious and exact
observation of which Tennyson is the perpetual
example, and of which, in our own time, both Mr.
Edmund Blunden and Mr. Robert Nichols have
provided interesting specimens. He rarely offers
us one of those phrases of half-a-dozen words
which stay in the memory because they are so
felicitous a description of something seen, such as
Tennyson's " like a downward smoke, the silver
stream," or Mr. Nichols's " the chill shower
brightens on the pane." There are a few such
felicities here and there in his work. " Lean-
stalked purple lavender " is one of them: " moulded
furze " perhaps, another. But in *The Linnet*,
whence comes the second of these two phrases,
the impression which is given to the reader of an
open, windy, sunny hillside is breathed out of the
whole poem rather than conveyed by any particular
stroke of it. He prefers, as a rule, the general
word; but it is his secret, as well as his peculiarity,
that he knows how to place it so as to secure a
particular effect. The value of the word " bright "
in the last line but one of the passage quoted from
The Bells is an instance of this; and here it is
obvious that " bright clouds " provides no definite
image by itself but only in the context where the
image is sharp enough.

If we pursue this brief study of Mr. de la Mare's
imagery into that part of his work where he describes
things and scenes which are not of ordinary
experience, it begins to be apparent that to make a

distinction here between fact and fancy may, if the effort be pressed too far, prove more misleading than serviceable. There is a country of his own creation, the counterpart of Xanadu, and the dim lake of Auber, and the misty mid-region of Weir, a world in which are to be found his Arabia and the house in *The Listeners* and his mountains " with frosty ulys overgrown "—a flower this last, by the way, which has been vainly looked for in text-books on Alpine botany, but which is a standing reminder of the poet's remarkable sense of words. These poems do seem, on the surface, to come from another source than those which have just been described. *The Bells* or *The Sunken Garden* might have had their origin in physical impressions. *Arabia* and *The Listeners* clearly cannot be anything but records of spiritual experiences, such experiences as may come to a feeling mind anywhere, lying awake in bed, or on the top of a mountain or on the top of a 'bus. But the actual result is in both cases the same. Whatever may have been the first incentive, whether something externally seen or heard, or only a movement in the mind, the expression is on the same plane of reality and truth. Compare with *The Bells* these lines of description from a poem of apparently different origin :—

" And he felt in his heart their strangeness,
    Their stillness answering his cry,
While his horse moved, cropping the dark turf,
    'Neath the starred and leafy sky.
    . . . Ay, they heard his foot upon the stirrup,
    And the sound of iron on stone,
And how the silence surged softly backward,
    When the plunging hoofs were gone."

The Poetry of Mr. Walter de la Mare

The experience, the mood, is made to take concrete form in these yet not too sharp details; but *The Bells* is also a mood, a spiritual experience. Both, by touches which are vivid and yet not too definite, disengage the magic which is Mr. de la Mare's peculiar property.

The power which we call "magic" proceeds from an inextricable combination of imagery and music: it is never found in a composition where both these characteristics are not remarkable. The pictures and sounds of which *Kubla Khan* and *Ulalume* are made up produce a quite definite effect on the mind; but it is easier to note this effect, and even to describe it, than to say precisely *how* it is produced. These are symbols and means of persuasion which address themselves immediately to the spirit and not by the ordinary methods of logical speech. Mr. de la Mare employs symbols of a like sort, not indeed to produce the same effect, but in the same manner. With him, as with Poe and Coleridge, sound and image can hardly be separated or made each to confess its share in the magic they together produce. But the effect and the beauty of his versification would be difficult to exaggerate. The various and subtle music of his verse is hardly to be paralleled in English literature except in the work of Campion and Mr. Bridges. Campion's rhythms are probably, to a great extent, the creations of a mind occupied with the composition of songs: they are sometimes almost unintelligible without the settings for which they were meant. Mr. Bridges's lovely and fruitful inventions are the result of intense conscious experiment, not the instinctive flowers of a mind struggling to express inspirations too subtle for any ordinary use of words. Mr. de la Mare has

77

not experimented with any new metres that can
be classified or reduced to a formula. His most
beautiful successes occur unexpectedly, inexplicably,
in the omission or the insertion of a syllable, by
methods which depend not on consideration but on
the spontaneous promptings of an ever fortunate
instinct:—

> " Far are the shades of Arabia,
>   Where the Princes ride at noon . . .
>
> Speak not—whisper not;
> Here bloweth thyme and bergamot. . . .
>
> ' I have no master,' said the Blind Boy,
>   ' My mother, "Dame Venus" they do call;
> Cowled in this hood, she sent me begging
>   For whate'er in pity may befall. . . .'
>
> See this house, how dark it is
> Beneath its vast-boughed trees! . . ."

It is true that Mr. de la Mare's range of rhythmical
possibilities is not very wide. There are certain
types of metre he has never attempted and which
he will never attempt. But within his range his
discoveries are almost infinitely various. A sufficiently elaborate system of metrical notation might
perhaps express the mechanical peculiarities of these
effects, and even show that there was very little
in them. But it could not explain their appropriate-
ness in each case, could not show us how to repro-
duce their charm; nor could it explain the many
instances in which there is no obvious mechanical
peculiarity, but where the rhythm is still plainly the
poet's own, expressing something which the mere

78

meanings of words could never have expressed. Before I leave this subject it seems worth while to add that, so far as I know, none of the many composers who have attempted to set Mr. de la Mare's verses has done that justice to his cadences which, I think, he would have had from the Elizabethan lutenists. I once heard a distinguished young musician restore regularity (at least I take it that must have been his intention) to the lovely line, " His lambs outnumber a noon's roses " by giving two notes to the word " noon's."

This is all very well; and if what I have said is true, Mr. de la Mare is a charming, a delightful, and an original poet. But I should like to claim something more for him than this. Let us make no mistake about it: beautiful imagery, beautiful music, even the " magic " which is compounded of them—these things, indispensable as such qualities may be, admirable and entertaining as they may be in themselves, do not give the utmost we demand from poetry unless they express something which is more than themselves. Here a certain complication enters into the argument, a complication which always enters into the criticism of poetry, because the poet's attitude towards his work necessarily differs from that of the reader. (A man may be, of course, and most men of poetic mind are, both poet and reader in respect of the same work; but this occurs at different times, and there is a fundamental difference between the two attitudes.) If I ascribe to the body of Mr. de la Mare's work a definitely edifying influence, I do not mean to suggest that the poet has ever had the remotest thought of edifying any one. His business, as poet, is to express a certain spirit; but if this expression be achieved, the influence of that spirit naturally emerges and presents itself to our estimation.

Matthew Arnold, in one of his essays, quotes a saying of Butler's that " endeavouring to enforce upon our own minds a practical sense of virtue, or to beget in others that practical sense of it which a man really has himself, is a virtuous *act*." In this sense there are a good many collections of verse which may be taken as the equivalent of so many virtuous lives; and these are the work of poets whose central and determining spirit is that of moral beauty, of, to use an uncompromising word, goodness. Let not this be taken as disparaging any poetry of which the same cannot be said. We have plenty of room in our capacity of appreciation for beauty of sight and sound, for tales well told, and for all the arts that are desirable only as means of entertainment. But we must admit the superior power of a poetry which does something, which urges us, though only by example and implicitly, not explicitly, towards better living. There is an ancient definition of an eloquent man as one who can persuade other men that he is likely to be right. So the best poet is he who can persuade us, not by preaching at us, not by reasoning with us, but by purely æsthetic means, by the expression of his temper in poetry, that his is a right temper, one which is conducive to the leading of a good life.

The spirit which Mr. de la Mare most frequently and most persuasively expresses in his work is one of kindness and pity. He is, in the first place, the poet of lost paradises. Almost all his poetry expresses dissatisfaction with this world, with this life, and a straining towards something more to be desired, which is indescribable, almost unimaginable,

of which an image is evoked as it were between the
words of his poems. If he has one constant and
recurring thought about the world it is this—that
there is a better place to be in than the one in which
we now find ourselves. Sometimes this paradise
lies back in childhood, sometimes forward or in
another world or undiscovered in the depths of
the human mind. He is like his own Rachel who—

> " Sings of hope
>   And of memories:
> Sings to the little
>   Boy that stands
> Watching those slim,
>   Light, heedful hands.
> He looks in her face;
>   Her dark eyes seem
> Dark with a beautiful
>   Distant dream."

Sometimes it is indeed no more than a dream which
will never be realised :—

> " Think! in Time's smallest clock's minutest beat
>   Might there not rest be found for wandering
>   feet ?
> Or, 'twixt the sleep and wake of Helen's dream,
> Silence wherein to sing love's requiem ?
> No, no. Nor earth, nor air, nor fire, nor deep
> Could lull poor mortal longingness asleep.
> Somewhere there Nothing is; and there lost
>   Man
> Shall win what changeless vague of peace he
>   can."

It is perhaps a little disconcerting to be reminded

by Mr. de la Mare of Baudelaire, whose surroundings and career, whose spirit and the expression of it, seem at first sight so utterly different. But he too, was a poet of lost paradises, though he strove to find a substitute for them in *les paradis artificiels.* He, too, gave voice continuously to the feeling that something was wanting in this life, that it would be better elsewhere—all that is for ever contained in the cry, " *Emporte-moi, wagon ! enlève-moi, frégate !* " And once in a singular and beautiful poem, written in a mood not very common in him, he expressed, I think, what is the secret of Mr. de la Mare's peculiar temper. The poem is called *Le Cygne.* It was suggested by the sight of an escaped swan; and it is Baudelaire's gesture of compassion towards all who, like himself, were exiles in this world:—

" Je pense à la négresse, amaigrie et phthisique,
  Piétinant dans la boue, et cherchant, l'œil hagard,
  Les cocotiers absents de la superbe Afrique
  Derrière la muraille immense du brouillard;

A quiconque a perdu ce qui ne se retrouve
  Jamais, jamais! à ceux qui s'abreuvent de pleurs
  Et tettent la Douleur comme une bonne louve!
  Aux maigres orphelins séchant comme des fleurs!

Ainsi dans la forêt où mon esprit s'exile
  Un vieux Souvenir sonne à plein souffle du cor!
  Je pense aux matelots oubliés dans une île,
  Aux captifs, aux vaincus! . . . à bien d'autres
    encor! "

Baudelaire melted for once; and his sense of exile awakened in him pity for those in a like case.

The Poetry of Mr. Walter de la Mare

Ordinarily it produced nothing but scorn for himself, for his fellow-sufferers, and, most of all, for the thick-skinned people who do not suffer. In Mr. de la Mare the feeling of pity is constant, and for him there is nobody who does not suffer: we are all where we ought not to be, we are all less happy than we should be, whether we know it or not.

It would be interesting, and no doubt edifying, to follow the up-shoots of this master inspiration all through his work ; but it would take far more space than can be found for it here. It can only be said that he expresses his own spirit, his own discoveries without any trace of argument or didacticism: his assumption that his is the lot of mankind is no more than implicit. But his sense of exile flowers again and again, in pity, in kindness, in humility—even in one of the loveliest poems he ever wrote, in gratitude for the loveliness of this world:—

> " What lovely things
>   Thy hand hath made:
> The smooth-plumed bird
>   In its emerald shade,
> The seed of the grass,
>   The speck of stone
> Which the wayfaring ant
>   Stirs—and hastes on!
>
> Though I should sit
>   By some tarn in thy hills,
> Using its ink
>   As the spirit wills
> To write of Earth's wonders,
>   Its live, willed things,

> Flit would the ages
>   On soundless wings
> Ere unto Z
>   My pen drew nigh;
> Leviathan told,
>   And the honey-fly:
> And still would remain
>   My wit to try—
> My worn reeds broken,
>   The dark tarn dry,
> All words forgotten—
>   Thou, Lord, and I."

That is grandeur, achieved not by " trying one's hand at the grand manner," but simply by humility and sincerity.

A well-meaning critic observed recently—apparently in extenuation—that no one but a fool would ask Mr. de la Mare to write an epic. He seems to have meant that Mr. de la Mare was well enough in his way, piping little hedgerow melodies, and that we ought not to despise him for doing no more. Well—if we use the word in its stricter sense, neither Mr. de la Mare nor any other man is likely to write an epic again till a new heroic age comes upon the earth. But if we understand by it, what this critic probably wished us to understand, a large poem of large pretensions, such as *The Prelude*, then I know of no man of his generation from whom such an attempt might, with better reason, be awaited with more excitement and interest. He has, much more than most of his contemporaries, a central conception underlying his work, not a code or a theory, but an idea, instinctive and native; and this conception is not eccentric or limited but applicable to the life of every one. His development in breadth and power has been continuous and rapid throughout the whole of his poetic career. *The Listeners*, published in 1912, showed a clear advance, not only in sureness but in depth, over the *Poems* of 1906; and *Motley* (1918) repeated and excelled that advance. In *The Veil* (1921), Mr. de la Mare's last volume, a curious quality is present. These poems suggest that so much new material has come to him as almost to throw him back into the position of a beginner—a beginner of much greater genius than the easy technician of *Motley*. He has become intermittently harsh and crabbed, sometimes even inexact and crude; but such faults suggest only that his advance is continuing with accelerated rapidity and with greater scope. These pieces are opening up new veins of thought, new modes of experience; and in the very awkwardness of some of them is betrayed the truly original poet's inability to stand still or to be content with doing again what he has already done well.

The Poetry of Mr. John Freeman

THERE have been periods in which it has been demanded of poetry only, or chiefly, that it should gratify the senses, that it should recall or suggest experiences of sight, touch, hearing, taste, or smell. In face of any such demand, the poetry of Mr. Freeman would have gone for lost, since, in addition to certain positive obstacles in the way of reading it, it would have suffered from the negative quality of offering no very strong invitation to surmount these obstacles. It is a poetry curiously devoid of sensual attraction; and even the music of the verse, which is always subtle and sometimes lovely, the creation of a patient and cunning prosodist, a thing by no means to be forgotten in any survey, is so tenuous and, as it were, so abstract as to reverberate rather in the mental than in the physical ear. Perhaps even now, in a generation not so exclusively devoted to colour and shape and bodily delights as have been at least some of its predecessors, this constitutes one of the greatest barriers in the way of a more general appreciation of Mr. Freeman's work.

His first book, *Twenty Poems*, was published in 1909, his second, *Fifty Poems*, the first to attract much notice, in 1911. Since then the recognition of his gifts has become more widely spread among poets and among critics, though not much more, it is probable, among other readers; and such recognition as there has been still suffers from a certain vagueness and perplexity, not clearly distinguishing his merits or separating them from his defects. The volume which forms the subject of

these pages[1] contains, apparently, all he has chosen
to preserve of both his earlier and his later work,
and is, in fact, a collected edition, by means of
which it is possible to survey his poetry as a whole.
Only thus indeed is it possible to make other than
groping and inaccurate comments on his characteristics. It has been remarked of his earlier and
less comprehensive books that it was necessary
to read each of them entire and in sequence. He,
more than most poets, suffers by the detachment
of single pieces; and very often such as are sufficiently near perfection, as wholes, to suffer least
by detachment are not among his most representative. He is an unequal writer; not all his poems,
especially the most ambitious, are evenly good
throughout; and fine and characteristic touches
occur in poems which are otherwise among his
worst. This large collection, containing nearly
two hundred titles, presents therefore a valuable
opportunity for estimating his excellences and his
faults and for attempting a coherent portrait of
him as a poet.

" The earlier pieces," he states correctly in the
note to this addition, " will easily be distinguished
by those who wish to distinguish them." Mr.
Freeman has changed, as he recognises, since the
publication of his first verses; but the change
seems to have been consistently in one direction,
and to have been the development of a germ not
hard to perceive in his beginnings. He is now,
so he describes himself:—

> " A man serious with change
> Of life and death,"

but his earliest work, in its already settled gravity,

[1] *Poems Old and New.* By John Freeman. (Selwyn and Blount.)

showed him capable of becoming, indeed by inward necessity certain to become, such a man. The change has been not in purpose but in experience and knowledge. He is more serious, in the common sense of the word, than most of our poets, serious enough to have been called a didactic. He has not merely a definite attitude towards life. That attitude is based upon certain definite principles to which he clings; and both attitude and principles are of a sort that prevents him from showing any levity, even that which arises out of sheer ecstatic joy in life. His attitude is necessarily implicit in the best and most characteristic of his compositions. It is his occasional defect that here and there his principles are somewhat too explicitly stated, in a manner which is not quite that of poetry.

The word " didactic " rings rather ominously in modern ears; and some consideration of its meaning is not out of place in studying Mr. Freeman's poetry. He is deeply moved by the contemplation of moral beauty, of the beauty of conduct in its widest sense, of man's relations with eternity; and these things are pictured in his verse in such a way that the reader may derive moral profit from them. But when we speak of " didactic poetry " we do not mean merely poetry from which we can learn something. We mean poetry the writer of which has definitely set out to teach us something; and our distrust of the term embodies our obscure understanding of the fact that in so doing the poet has refused his proper function and has offered us what we do not ask from him. For it is poetry that must teach us, not the poet: the poet must bear witness to the truth, not expound it. His work must be the outcome of delight in the perception of the truth's existence, not of any desire to impart it or even to make it prevail. The poet, in a word, while and in so far as he is a poet, must be absolutely disinterested. If he loses this mood, he enters into that of the preacher whose function it is to inculcate and to expound.

Hence it is that so much of the "didactic" poetry of the eighteenth and nineteenth centuries, from rhymed essays on morals to studies in the philosophy of evolution, has rightly fallen into discredit. This is not poetry but the statement in metre of philosophical notions. And, by intending what he should not, the poet fails in what he intends. Poetry, he knows, is the highest expression of humanity and can convey truth absolutely as no other medium can convey it. But "truth of science does not become truth of religion until it is made religious"; and similarly truth of no sort, religious or scientific or philosophical, becomes truth of poetry until it is made poetical, until, that is to say, it is exposed to the fusing heat of contemplative ecstasy which is the specific and indispensable condition of poetic creation. When this is absent, the truth escapes the clumsy attempt to state it in bare terms; and the result is something which is not poetry, and which, as a rule, only suffers by being presented with pseudo-poetic trappings and circumstance.

It is thus not hard to see why the error of didacticism is one to which the most ambitious and most earnest poets are especially liable. The timid and self-restricting writer may avoid it, but not one who seeks to go deep. Neither Shelley nor Milton is entirely free from it; and Keats almost dimmed the radiance of more than one of his loveliest compositions by stating a "moral" too baldly. These lapses are evidences of the writer's

failure perfectly to fuse his content, in the strictest
sense, and his form, in the widest sense, which
fusion is the last and the highest of the problems
confronting the poet. It is clear that the more
elevated and abstract the attempted content becomes,
the more difficult will be the process of fusion; and
to produce specimens of this failure from Mr.
Freeman's work is only to rank him with those
whose intentions at least have been of a noble sort.
Mr. Freeman has other characteristics and other
faults; but this trait of didacticism must be considered first. Take, for example, these lines from
Judgment Day:—

" It was not in these bodies that we drew
  Near, nearer: never, never by these we knew
  Transfusion past all sense of ' I ' and ' You.'

It was youth's blindness held the body so dear:
  Slowly, slowly, year after bewildered year,
  The dark thinned and the eyes of love grew
      clear."

This is a proposition, debatable or acceptable, but
it is hardly poetry—it is argument. The fusion
has not been effected: the writer is in the preacher's
mood, not in that of contemplative ecstasy. But
the conclusion of the same poem is a sufficient
contrast, differing from the preceding passage in
kind, not in degree:—

                              " Even now,
  Though body, to body submissively still bow,
  'Tis not on body's blood that our loves grow.

The Poetry of Mr. John Freeman

Though I am old and you are old, though nerves
Slacken and beauty slowly loses its curves,
And greedy Time the bone and sinew starves,

Like some lean Captain gloating over a town
That has not fallen, but will fall, every stone
O'erthrust and every bravery overthrown;

Who entering the defeated walls at last
Finds emptiness, and hears an escaping blast,
Triumphant from the shining east hills cast,

And knows defeat in victory. . . . O that rare
Music is ours, is ours—prelusive air
Caught from the Judgment music high and
    severe.

Will it indeed be thus ? Yes, thus! The body
    burns,
Not with desire and into pale smoke turns,
And there is only flame towards flame that
    yearns.

While that ill lecherous Time among the stones
Sits musing and rocking his old brittle bones,
Irked by long shadows, mocked by those bright
    far tones."

This passage is indeed open to exception in minutiæ
(the third terzet, for example, is too diffuse compared
with the rest of the simile), but it achieves what the
other did not; and the difference between the two
is precisely that in the first the writer is still
expounding his idea, while in the second he has
become absorbed by the contemplation of it and
has found for it a true and poetical symbol, has

become, in fact, what he was not before—a poet.
The contrast here displayed illustrates our argument;
and it might be paralleled a great many times from
Mr. Freeman's work. Sometimes, as in *The Human
Music*, the idea comes limping at the end of the
composition, a jejune and untransfigured moral.
This poem is the spiritual biography of a soul dis-
mayed by the harshness and evil of the world; and
frequently in the course of it absorption in detail
produces the right poetical mood. But the last
lines, which should sum up and unite the total
impression of what precedes them, are sheer
deception in their fall below the proper temperature.
The idea is definite enough and is conveyed to the
reader, but this conclusion makes it clear that the
writer has not succeeded in conceiving it as a poet:—

" Kindness gave solitude the lovely light
　　She loved, and made less terrible black midnight.
　　Even as a bird its unlearned music pours
　　Though windows all be blind and shut the doors,
　　And sings on still though no faint sound be
　　　　heard
　　But wind and leaves and another lonely bird:
　　So poured she untaught kindness all around
　　And in that human music comfort found—
　　Music her own and music heard from others,
　　Prime music of all lovers, children, mothers,
　　Precarious music between all men sounding,
　　The horror of silent and dark Powers con-
　　　　founding.
　　Singing that music she could bravely live;
　　Hearing it, find less sorrow to forgive."

Sometimes, as in *The Song of the Forest*, an ode on
the conclusion of the war, the right mood finds
92

success not in the employment of a symbol but purely in the potency of chosen and austere diction:

" I cannot syllable that unworded praise—
    An ashen sapling bending in Thy wind,
    Uplifting in Thy light new-budded leaves;
    Nor for myself nor any other raise
    My boughs in music, though the woodland
        heaves—
    O with what ease of pain at length resigned,
    What hope to the old inheritance restored!
    Thy praise it is that men at last are glad.
    Long unaccustomed brightness in their eyes
    Needs must seem beautiful in thine, bright Lord.
    And to forget the part that sorrow had
    In every shadowed breast, where still it lies,
    Is there not praise in such forgetfulness?
    For to grieve less means not that love is less."

This is a noble thought, expressed, as every poetical thought must be expressed, so that we feel that in no other way could it have been communicated to us immediately and without impairment. And it is precisely this which we ask of poetry and which distinguishes poetry from any other form of human activity.

But the rare moments in which Mr. Freeman reaches his highest level of achievement are not, and could hardly be, unexpected, unrelated and inexplicable leaps into the blue. They rise from a mass of verse which is not by any means made up (though what I have written so far might possibly give that impression) of failures so to rise. His finest poems result from the contemplation of wide and deep ideas, but they have a necessary background of poems resulting from the contemplation of ideas less wide and less deep, or of sensations only. This poetry has an individual body as well as soul: it has, that is to say, its own particular range of symbol and imagery. Moreover, it has as a whole a quite unusual unity and coherence. It is almost a single work, a sequence of poems rather than a collection of disparate pieces; and the verses of less importance exist in easily perceptible relations with those of greater importance. It is therefore convenient to consider the general questions of style and manner all together at this point.

A very few of the pieces in the third part of the volume, which contains Mr. Freeman's early work, show recognisable signs of derivation. Here is a sonnet which has traces of resemblance to Meredith, and here a song in whose cadences there is an Elizabethan echo. But, for the most part, Mr. Freeman's juvenilia are distinguished from his later work chiefly by the fact that in them he has not yet thoroughly explored or mastered his own powers. There are here not so many of the highest moments, and the lesser moments are, on the whole, not so intensely rendered; but between the third part of the book and the first there is little change of spirit or temper and very little of method.

His technique, which was never conventional, has never become revolutionary. His verse adheres to the iambic norm, but is subject to wide departures from it. It is fluid, flexible, and variable, undergoing changes and modulations in obedience to the writer's mood. It is mostly rhymed verse; but the rhyme counts in it for curiously little. Mr. Freeman is never a precisian in this matter. He is often content with the repetition of a word or with an assonance; or on occasion he lets the rhyme go by altogether. But even when his verse

is rhymed in the strictest and most formal way,
the actual ring of the rhymes plays only a small
part in its music. It is rather a thread holding the
poem together as unobtrusively as possible, than
a conspicuous element in its structure; and as a
rule Mr. Freeman contrives that even this function
shall be filled by the least number of rhymes,
securing his musical effects, and building up his
stanzas, by other means, as in the subtle though
unpretentious stanza-form of *Nightfall*:—

> " Eve goes slowly
>   Dancing lightly
> Clad with shadow up the hills;
>   Birds their singing
>   Cease at last, and silence
> Falling like fine rain the valley fills."

Such original forms, not all as successful as this,
are numerous in his work; and the general effect
produced is that of a subordination of rhyme a little
unexpected in any verse where it is retained at all.
Strong, full, and just rhyming has always been
considered an important part of the technique of
an English poet; and the habitual inaudibility of
Mr. Freeman's rhymes may be thought a sign of
technical weakness in him. It seems to me, however, that this quality cannot be separated from the
peculiar nature of his verse, the capacity of which
for beauty of sound is shown in *The Alde*, one of
the quietest and most lovely of his poems:—

> " How near I walked to Love,
>   How long, I cannot tell.
> I was like the Alde that flows
> Quietly through green level lands,

95

So quietly, it knows
Their shape, their greenness and their shadows
    well;
And then undreamingly for miles it goes
And silently, beside the sea.

Seamews circle over,
The winter wildfowl wings,
Long and green the grasses wave
Between the river and the sea.
The sea's cry, wild or grave,
From bank to low bank of the river rings;
But the uncertain river though it crave
The sea, knows not the sea.

Was that indeed salt wind ?
Came that noise from falling
Wild waters on a stony shore ?
Oh, what is this new troubling tide
Of eager waves that pour
Around and over, leaping, parting, recalling ? ...
How near I moved (as day to same day wore)
And silently, beside the sea! "

It is certain in any case that this fact helps to
produce the general air of remoteness and absence
of sensuous appeal in Mr. Freeman's work, which
is also produced by the character of his imagery.
Like so many of his generation, he draws the most
part of his imagery from English country scenes;
but his countryside is one that he has transfigured
and made peculiar to himself. He does not describe
what he himself calls :—

" Such easy brightness as the poets see,
    Or easy gloom or hues of faerie."

The Poetry of Mr. John Freeman

His landscape, even when it is recognisably an English field or orchard such as we all know, is wilder and lonelier, and its atmosphere colder and rarer, than in the work of other poets. He seems instinctively to prefer evening and early morning to noon, the first days of spring and the last of autumn to high summer, buds to full flowers and leaves, and the flowers of April to the bolder-hued flowers of July. It is characteristic in him to be more vivid and concrete than usually elsewhere in such a picture as this:—

" On the wide fields the water gleams like snow
And snow like water pale beneath pale sky,
When old and burdened the pale clouds are
    stooped low.
Sudden as thought or startled bird's near cry
The whiteness of first light on hills of snow
New dropped from skiey hills of tumbling white
Streams from the ridge to where the long woods
    lie;
And tall ridge-trees lift their soft crowns of
    white
Above slim bodies all black or flecked with snow.
By the tossed foam of the not yet frozen brook
Black pigs go straggling over fields of snow;
The air is full of snow, and starling and rook
Are blacker amid the myriad streams of light."

This, from a recent poem, is inimitable in the exactness of the detail and in the breadth of suggestion which each trait brings to the whole. The same power is discernible, in varying degrees of accomplishment, in earlier poems, written when Mr. Freeman was more often content simply to record the moment's sensation. The lyrics, *Stone*

97

Trees, describing a sudden lightning flash in a
dark night, *It Was the Lovely Moon*:—

> " She lifted
> Slowly her white brow among
> Bronze cloud-waves that ebbed and drifted
> Faintly, faintlier afar."

The Yew, a dark shadow in the moonless garden,
November Skies, and half a dozen more might be
cited as exquisite pieces of work in this kind. But,
while Mr. Freeman's seriousness has deepened so
that he less often describes only the moment, yet
his power of description has grown at the same
time. Among the hitherto unpublished pieces,
The Ash has beautiful passages; and in *The
Unloosening*, a symbolic painting of the defeat of
Winter, there is an intensity of feeling and realisation greater perhaps than in any of the earlier
poems:—

> " . . . He saw all the laughing valley,
>   Heard the unloosened waters leaping down
> Broadening over the meadows; saw the sun
>   running
>   From hill to hill and glittering upon the town.
>
> All day he stared. But his head drooped at
>   evening,
>   Bent and slow he stumbled into the white
> Cavern of a great chalk hill, hedged with tall
>   bushes,
>   And in its darkness found a darker night.
>
> Among the broken cliff and falling water,
>   Freezing or falling quietly everywhere;

Locked in a long, long sleep, his brain un-
     dreaming,
   With only water moving anywhere.

Old men at night dreamed that they saw him
     going,
   And looked, and dared not look, lest he should
     turn,
And young men felt the air beating on their
     bodies,
   And the young women woke from dreams
     that burn.

And children going through the field at morning
   Saw the unloosened waters leaping down,
And broke the hazel boughs and wore the tassels
   Above their eyes—a pale and shaking crown."

This power of describing landscape constitutes
perhaps not the highest, but certainly the broadest
appeal of Mr. Freeman's poetry. The infallible
working of the instinctive preferences, to which I
have already alluded, contributes strongly to the
effect of unity which his work produces and makes
as a background for his thoughts and feeling an
identifiable, consistent, and unique countryside.

The main characteristics of his style, as I have
just described them, may suggest as a predominant
impression that Mr. Freeman, with his ascetic
rather than sensuous verse, his bleak rather than
ascetic imagery, is essentially a poet of the spirit
and not of the flesh. Poetry is indeed so indefeasibly a spiritual exercise that this distinction is
doubtful and difficult to make; but it may be
allowed to stand for what it suggests, if it be not
taken as a literal statement. His poems are, in

fact, records of the adventures of a soul ; and it is not unfitting to use the phrase Goethe used of of his own work and to say that they are fragments of a confession. This is not the confession of a man with Goethe's comprehensive mind or his insatiable desire for something of all knowledge and all experience; but it recounts, however brokenly, the reactions towards, and the speculations on, life of a mind perpetually engrossed by the problem of the existence of the human spirit in the world and perpetually revolving this problem, within a comparatively narrow range of experience but with a real intensity and seriousness of application.

This view of his work embraces the whole of his book with its two hundred pieces; and naturally only a cursive and selective summary under this aspect is possible. As a psychologist, an inquirer into the motions of the individual heart, he expresses himself especially in two sequences of poems in the second part of his collection, *Memories of Childhood* and *Wild Heart*, which are in many ways characteristic of his attitude towards the world. The first is a confession which depicts the initiation of the child into the world, the child's pleasures, discoveries, glimpses of beauty and disappointments, and ends with the thought:—

" Hateful it seems now, yet was I not happy ? . . .
Who may regret what was, since it has made
Himself himself ?   All that I was I am,
And the old childish joy now lives in me
At sight of a green field or a green tree."

Wild Heart is the confession of a grown man in the presence of love, the confession of a meta-physical poet who has not perhaps Donne's lightness or agility of thought, but who certainly has Donne's determination to pluck the reality, if possible, out of deceptive and confusing shows:—

> " Come not to me,
>   Bring not your body nearer,
> Though you overleapt the miles
>   I could not behold you clearer.'

It is in form a statement, but in fact an inquiry. Such poetic mood as is here attained springs from the contemplation rather of the paradox than of the elusive and bewildering truth. It is often so with Mr. Freeman; and perhaps this too plays its part in giving him his preponderating air of earnestness instead of the lightness and serenity of the poets who see immediately, or believe that they see, an immediate truth.

But he goes further than, and generalises from, his own experiences; and not the least interesting part of his work is the frequency in it of generalisations on the life of man and his place in the universe. It is rich in such gnomic lines as this, of the flocks and herds:—

> " Earth's chosen nourished by earth's wise
>   self-chosen."

And the first part of the collection contains two long poems, *Beechwood* and *Out of the East*, which at least indicate a grandiose widening of theme. The second of these is perhaps a failure. It is too diffuse and too rambling; and the author seems throughout the most of it to have allowed its breadth of subject to distract him from the narrow and precise task of finding the only right word for each occasion.

First Essays on Literature

Nevertheless, its subject, as well as its length, makes it the most considerable and ambitious attempt on which Mr. Freeman has yet entered; and in an age whose poets are most justly reproached with timidity in the choice of subjects this is a fact not to be neglected. It describes the conflict of tradition and change, of age and youth, in a primitive tribe in the beginnings of humanity:—

" When man first walked upright and soberly
    Reflecting as he paced to and fro."

The old prince and his grandson are returning from the burial of the boy's father, killed in the prime of life while hunting. The old man explains how the snapping of this link has cut him off from a new world which he understands only enough to fear it. They go into their house and go to sleep; but both lie awake dreaming, the old man of dangers approaching the tribe:—

" And all unsatisfied his people grown
    Would move from this rejected mountain
      range
  By yearlong valley journeys slowly down,
    Sun-following, till surfeited with change,
  Mid idle pastures pitched or fabled town,
    Subdued to climes and kings and customs
      strange,
  At length their very name should die away
  And all their remnant be a vague ' Men say.' "

the younger of a time when he would lead out his people to new greatness. The thing is not perfectly done, but it is a fine conception, and it is in some ways characteristic of Mr. Freeman's habitual thought.

The Poetry of Mr. John Freeman

For, if he is to be described as a nature-poet, it is because he sees humanity as though it were a forest-god only half escaped from the tree. Nature is always present in his poems, but now as an influence on mankind, now as a symbol of it. He speaks of " the world that is the changing image of my thought "; but it is for him a framework as well as an image. This fact is to be taken as the centre of his work; and if it is a conception that he has so far expressed only fragmentarily, yet the fact that he has expressed it even so much entitles him to be taken seriously as a poet.

Mr. Masefield: Some Characteristics

IT may be true that there is a small circle of readers and critics by whose opinion reputations are made. It is quite certain that the reputations which seem to be made there have a way of escaping the control of their putative creators. Nine years ago Mr. Masefield published *The Everlasting Mercy* in the *English Review*. Before he did so his name was known to a comparatively small number of persons who regarded him with some admiration and more curiosity; but afterwards he received fame instead of expectant attention. For some time he bulked large in two worlds. He made modern poetry popular before Rupert Brooke; and critical opinion, broadly speaking, agreed in owning the novelty and ambition of his work and the adequacy of his talents. In the theatre he seemed to be the inheritor of Synge, destined to make Synge's methods his own on a larger scale and before a wider audience. Mr. John Galsworthy, then at the zenith of a reputation which has followed a somewhat similar course, proclaimed him " the man of the hour, and the man of to-morrow, too, in poetry and the play-writing craft." At the universities, among the rising generation, his name had great power; and a new book by him was genuinely an event of importance. Elderly and academic persons confirmed his adherents by attacking him on the ground that he was coarse, violent, gratuitously ugly, that he chose subjects unfitted for poetry— charges which, as they were preferred, were insufficient and might be cheerfully accepted as a challenge. For a little while it really seemed to many that a

Mr. Masefield : Some Characteristics

new writer had emerged of the rare stature and originality which engage the interest both of the general public and of the sceptical and selective readers who attempt to anticipate the judgment of their descendants.

But I do not think that this is true any longer. Mr. Masefield's works were not found wanting in the qualities at first discerned in them. But radical defects, which had hitherto somehow escaped general notice, were revealed; and some of the very qualities turned out, on cooler examination, not to have the value with which they had been credited. Worse still, the defects became apparent through, as it were, a sort of rash on the surface, an outcrop of awkwardnesses and ineptitudes which lent themselves quite charmingly to ridicule. The public continued to admire, possibly even more than ever; but first one voice was raised among the critics, then another and another.

In this swing of opinion there is some danger that Mr. Masefield's real achievements may be overlooked; and the danger continues so long as his demerits are not clearly stated. The general public, once he had been forced on its notice, liked him to a considerable extent for excellent reasons. The general public does indeed like good qualities in, for instance, Shakespeare, Scott, and Dickens, and even in its unworthy favourites, in cheap and trashy novelists, it has a way of feeling after virtues which better writers would be better for possessing. Mr. Masefield actually has originality, enterprise, ambition, and some degree of force: he is one of the most interesting figures in modern literature. Assuming that he has genius, that he did not capture opinion only by pretence, the mere range of his work must be considered and may be reckoned to his credit. He has experimented in many forms He has written lyrics and sonnets and a series of successful narrative poems, plays both in prose and in verse which have stood the test of production, several novels and collections of stories, a book on Shakespeare, and books about the war. His sincerity as an artist may often be questioned, will certainly be questioned in the pages that follow; but his personal sincerity, in the broadest and most fundamental sense, is beyond doubt. If he has pandered to anything, it has been to his own mistaken artistic ambitions, not to the taste of the public which admires him. His work, now considerable in bulk as well as wide in range, is almost all thoroughly characteristic, almost all shot with virtues and vices, almost all offering substantial material for the process of sifting and distinction which must assuredly be applied to it. It is more than worth while, it is important, that the attempt should be made to distinguish between the virtues for which he will be remembered and the vices which, on discovery, rendered his critical following so profoundly distrustful, if not completely disillusioned.

Mr. Masefield's earliest work is a tangle of influences and themes; and its most interesting characteristic was the way in which these were combined. He had experience of ships and the sea, knowledge and love of English country, and the beginnings of a view of life; and he expressed the themes thus suggested to him in a manner reminiscent of Mr. Yeats, with occasional assistance from Mr. Kipling. One opens his second book, *Ballads*, to find the following lines:—

Mr. Masefield: Some Characteristics

" Would I could win some quiet and rest, and a
    little ease,
In the cool gray hush of the dusk, in the dim
    green place of the trees,
Where the birds are singing, singing, singing,
    crying aloud
The song of the red, red rose that blossoms
    beyond the seas."

One turns over a few pages and discovers *Cargoes*,
that celebrated poem without a finite verb, of which
the first verse describes a " quinquereme of Nine-
veh," and the second a " stately Spanish galleon,"
and the third a

" Dirty British coaster with salt-caked smoke stack
  Butting through the Channel in the mad March
    days,
  With a cargo of Tyne coal,
  Road-rails, pig-lead,
  Firewood, ironware, and cheap tin trays.

Subject, rhythm, and implication are alike derived
from Mr. Kipling; and the first feelings of a reader
who saw these two passages in juxtaposition might
be wondering respect for a writer who could quench
his thirst at two so dissimilar springs.

His first prose shows traces of an influence not
so incompatible with that of Mr. Yeats. Just as
Synge had so used the peasant speech of the west
of Ireland as to create from it a medium of expression for poetry of a highly cultured sort, keeping
its flavour and yet turning it into the channels of
civilised literature, so Mr. Masefield attempted
to manipulate the language of old seamen telling
fo'c'sle yarns. The prose of *A Mainsail Haul* is

by no means merely reported dialect. It is a finished literary product in which fo'c'sle expressions and turns of speech are worked up on paper by a man of letters into rhythms no less cunning and refined than those of Pater or Wilde. Take this, from *A Sailor's Yarn*:—

" Now the next morning that fellow Bill I told you of was tacking down the city to the boat, singing some song or another. And when he got near to the jetty he went fumbling in his pocket for his pipe, and what should he find but a silver dollar that had slipped away and been saved. So he thinks: ' If I go aboard with this dollar, why the hands'll laugh at me; besides it's a wasting of it not to spend it.' So he cast about for some place where he could blue it in.

" Now close by where he stood there was a sort of great store, kept by a Johnny Dago. And if I was to tell you of the things they had in it I would need nine tongues and an oiled hinge to each of them. But Billy walked into this store, into the space inside, into like the 'tween decks, for to have a look about him before buying. And there were great bunches of bananas a-ripening against the wall. And sacks of dried raisins, and bags of dried figs, and melon seeds and pomegranates enough to sink you. Then there were cotton bales, and calico, and silk of Persia. And rum in puncheons and bottled ale. And all manner of sweets and a power of a lot of chemicals. And anchors gone rusty, fished up from the bay after the ships were gone. And spare cables, all ranged for letting go. And ropes and sails and balls of marline stuff. Then there was blocks of all kinds, wood and iron. Dunnage there was, and scantling, likewise sea-chests with pictures on them. And casks of beef and pork, and paint, and peas, and peterolium. But for not one of these things did Billy care a handful of bilge."

It must be conceded that this passage is vivid, if it is also a trifle " mannered "; and to be successful in this sort of writing is to show proof of a quality comparable to that which in sculpture would be called " sense of the material." Even the catalogue, an extremely literary device, is put with propriety into the mouth of the sailor and serves not as mere decoration but to display his gusto in the story. Here Mr. Masefield has converted his raw material into literature without destroying its character. The danger of the method, a danger from which even Synge did not wholly escape, is that the writer is tempted to charge his medium with more than it can bear, until nothing is left of its original character but a forced and false quaintness. This happens in *Port of Many Ships*, when another old sailor is made to say, describing the Day of Judgment:—

" The sun will just be setting in the sea, far away to the west, like a ball of red fire. And just as the curve of it goes below the sea, it will stop sinking and lie there like a door. And the stars and the earth and the wind will stop. And there will be nothing but the sea, and this red arch of the sun and the whales with the wrecks and a stream of light upon the water."

Overcharging of the material, the imposition of too severe a strain on his means of expression—these will perhaps be found to be Mr. Masefield's most damaging errors in compositions of greater extent and weight than the sketches of *A Mainsail Haul.*

So far the main element of individuality that we have discovered in Mr. Masefield's work has been in his choice of subjects and in his application of style to subject—a matter of importance, for, with a writer of any personality, the possession of a definite and favourite range of themes will, in the long run, determine style, drawing whatever may be original out of a chaos of echoes and influences. When Mr. Masefield began writing more ambitious compositions than his early songs and sketches he showed himself concerned with making poetry out of more or less contemporary life, the life of English peasants and labourers, and English seamen. His *Tragedy of Nan,* which was produced in 1908, is enacted in "a kitchen in the house of a small tenant farmer at Broad Oak on Severn"; and though the period is 1810 and the action turns on the crime of sheep-stealing, yet another year and another crime might have been substituted without great difficulty. The dialogue and action are for all practical purposes drawn from contemporary life; and the period actually chosen affords only minor convenience to the dramatist. In the series of narrative poems one describes the conversion of an evil-living poacher, another the ruin of a decent young labourer by a vile woman, another the contest between a wastrel and a serious farmer for a woman's love, another the attempt of a gentle artist to make himself a sailor among sailors. The hero of the latest of the series, *Reynard the Fox,* is no longer human; but there is a human background and the manner of the whole is as contemporary and human as that of its predecessors.

The early narratives were at first condemned for

their coarseness and violence and ugliness. Saul Kane prefaced his salvation by a bout of swearing, a prize-fight, a debauch, and a delirious fit of destruction in the streets of a country town. The story of Jim and Ern and Anna, in the *Widow in the Bye Street*, was a sordid business, a police-gazette affair, and so was that of Michael and Lionel and Mary in *The Daffodil Fields*. The story of Nan was not much better; she poisoned her rival with a pasty of tainted mutton and stabbed her faithless lover with a carving-knife. Worse, the incidental detail was often made up of ugly things. One critic complained of the fairmen, in *The Widow in the Bye Street*:—

" The dawn finds them filling empty cans
    In some sweet-smelling dusty country lane,
    Where a brook chatters over rusty pans."

He preferred that brooks, in poetry at least, should chatter over cress and decorative water-flowers. But the grave protests and accusations which greeted these poems when they first appeared were mostly based on wrong grounds. There is no subject which is unfit for poetry; all depends on what the poet makes of his subject. And, though it is no innovation to treat of contemporary life in verse, yet Mr. Masefield should have been commended for his effort to achieve an always useful and difficult thing. It was not from the conception that his errors sprang, but from the treatment.

Some of these errors are obvious on the surface. Mr. Masefield's sense of humour has never been strong enough to save him from destructive self-parodies. Even in *Reynard the Fox* the description

of Bunny Manor sounds like a malicious comment
on the succession of his early heroes:—

> " He too (a year before) had had
>   A taste for going to the bad."

And in *The Cold Cotswolds*, one of the most surprising pieces ever seriously put forth by a serious
writer, the poet retails horrors with the complacent
absurdity of a nonsense-rhyme:—

> " They hanged Will
>   As Will said;
> With one thrill
>   They choked him dead.
>
> Jane walked the wold
>   Like a gray gander;
> All grown old,
>   She would wander.
>
> She died soon:
>   At high tide,
> At full moon,
>   Jane died.

Besides this, he is too often a slack and inefficient
craftsman, too often allows himself to pass loosely
aimed words and forced rhymes of the most disconcerting sort. He is capable of saying that a
fox, in a tight corner, " did not blench." In
Biography, in the excellent episode of the boat-race,
he writes:—

> " 'Damn it, come on now.' 'On now,' 'On
>   now,' ' Starboard.'

'Port Fore,' 'Up with her, Port'; each
    cutter harboured
Ten eye-shut painsick strugglers."

Here ten per cent. of the effect of the word
"harboured" goes to sustaining some sort of a
place in the sense of the narrative, and ninety per
cent. to providing an atrociously ingenious rhyme
for "starboard"—a wrong proportion. Or he
writes:—

> "And then I met her friend,
>   Down by the water,
> Who cried, ' She's met her end,
>   That gray-eyed daughter.'"

where one is not sure whether the last word should
be taken as a forced rhyme or as a grotesque
affectation. Of the same order of insufficient
thought and scamped workmanship is the letter
in *Rosas*, written to his mother by a son who is
running away from home:—

> "'Dear mother,' said the letter, ' You and I
>   With different souls must live by different laws.
> I give back all you gave me, now good-bye.
>   If I go naked hence, you know the cause.
> I keep my father's name. When I am gone
> I shall be gone for ever. I am, John.'"

Here the signature is merely the bastard result
of a compromise between pure realism and the
conventional poetic rendering of ordinary speech—
a compromise dictated apparently by the necessities
of the metre—and it is destructive of all illusion.

    These defects, as I have said, are obvious, in

their causes and effects, on the surface. But what is more serious is that the reader of Mr. Masefield's poems, and indeed of almost all he has written, however much he may be captivated by the vigour of the narrative and the fresh vividness of the scenes presented, finds himself frequently checked by a strong sense of incongruity, amounting to falsity. When Saul Kane comes down from the hill with his brutal companions, after the fight, he sees:—

> " All the graves of all the ghosts
>   Who rise on Christmas Eve in hosts
>   To dance and carol in festivity
>   For joy of Jesus Christ's Nativity
>   (Bell-ringer Dawe and his two sons
>   Beheld 'em from the bell-tower once),
>   Two and two about about
>   Singing the end of Advent out,
>   Dwindling down to windlestraws
>   When the glittering peacock craws,
>   As craw the glittering peacock should
>   When Christ's own star comes over the wood.
>   Lamb of the sky come out of fold
>   Wandering windy heavens cold."

Throughout this passage it is impossible to resist the feeling that the voice is changing, until the last three lines are frankly impossible in the mouth of Saul Kane, converted though he be when he tells the story. Another striking, though minute, instance is to be found in *The Daffodil Fields* when the dying farmer confesses to his friends that:—

" I leave not even a farthing to my lovely son."

Mr. Masefield: Some Characteristics

Here again, though only for the space of one word, another voice speaks through the mouth of Nicholas Gray. It is the same in *The Tragedy of Nan*, when the heroine says:—

" There be three times, Dick, when no woman can speak. Beautiful times. When 'er 'ears 'er lover, and when 'er gives 'erself, and when 'er little one is born."

The cultured accent is disguised, the aitches are dropped, but the voice is the voice of the literary person not of the tragic peasant-girl.

These three instances have all been taken from the mouths of characters; and they are bad in the first place because they are not consonant with the persons on whom they are fathered. But an equal incongruity is often visible when the poet is speaking in his own person, in such lines as these from *The Widow in the Bye Street*:—

" ' Anna, I love you, and I always shall.'
He looked towards Plaister's End beyond Cot
    Hills.
A white star glimmered in the long canal,
A droning from the music came in thrills.
Love is a flame to burn out human wills,
Love is a flame to set the will on fire,
Love is a flame to cheat men into mire."

Apart from their intrinsic vagueness and emptiness, the last three lines are an abrupt and awkward departure from the key in which the whole narrative is set. They produce an effect as of a vision suddenly blurred or of the substitution of a picture for a real scene. The poet ceases to regard his theme directly; something is interposed between it and him.

The pity is that in direct vision he can be so good. The poem *Biography* contains many vivid and moving passages. The boat-race has already been cited for a blemish; but, taken as a whole, it is lively, convincing, and truthful.

" Days of endeavour have been good: the days
   Racing in cutters for the comrade's praise.
   The day that led my cutter at the turn,
   Yet could not keep the lead, and dropped astern;
   The moment in the spurt when both boats' oars
   Dipped in each other's wash, and throats grew
      hoarse,
   And teeth ground into teeth, and both strokes
      quickened
   Lashing the sea, and gasps came, and hearts
      sickened,
   And coxswains damned us, dancing, banking
      stroke,
   To put our weights on, though our hearts were
      broke,
   And both boats seemed to stick and sea seemed
      glue,
   The tide a mill race we were struggling through;
   And every quick recover gave us squints
   Of them still there, and oar-tossed water-glints,
   And cheering came, our friends, our foemen
      cheering,
   A long, wild, rallying murmur on the hearing,
   ' Port Fore! ' and ' Starboard Fore! ' ' Port
      Fore,' ' Port Fore,'
   ' Up with her,' ' Starboard '; and at that each oar
   Lightened, though arms were bursting, and eyes
      shut,

And the oak stretchers grunted in the strut,
And the curse quickened from the cox, our bows
Crashed, and drove talking water, we made vows,
Chastity vows and temperance; in our pain
We numbered things we'd never eat again
If we could only win; then came the yell
'Starboard,' 'Port Fore,' and then a beaten bell
Rung as for fire to cheer us. 'Now.' Oars bent,
Soul took the looms now body's bolt was spent,
'Damn it, come on now.' 'On now,' 'On
    now,' 'Starboard.'
'Port Fore,' 'Up with her, Port'; each cutter
    harboured
Ten eye-shut painsick strugglers, 'Heave, oh
    heave,'
Catcalls waked echoes like a shrieking sheave.
'Heave,' and I saw a back, then two. 'Port
    Fore,'
'Starboard,' 'Come on'; I saw the midship
    oar,
And knew we had done them. 'Port Fore,'
    'Starboard,' 'Now.'
I saw bright water spurting at their bow,
Their cox full face an instant. They were done.
The watchers' cheering almost drowned the gun.
We had hardly strength to toss our oars; our cry
Cheering the losing cutter was a sigh."

These lines constitute a piece of lively and economical
description; but they are more than that, they are
the rendering of a spiritual experience. Mr. Masefield does here, without effort, without straining,
without falsity, as fine a thing as he ever set out to
do, and this without using even a sentence of
general reflection. It is the same in *Dauber*, in the
passages which describe the rounding of the Horn

and the expected entry into harbour. It is the same, though in a quite different sort, in the *Tragedy of Nan*, when Dick Gurvil, with a few sentences about cider and cakes, fixes his character definitely and inalterably in the mind. Such are the passages which we have to set against those already quoted.

It is probably in the contrast thus marked that the secret of Mr. Masefield's recurrent weakness is to be discovered. He is a writer with great powers of description, knowledge of the world and of the people in it, an excellent fund of material, and a strong sense of the immortal and tragic issues which underlie the movements of human beings. But this last, which most inspires him when he is least actively aware of it, seems to disable him when it enters the field of his consciousness. A wise critic said years ago, unavailingly, that we ought to take pains to avoid making Mr. Masefield self-conscious. When he is not conscious of himself as interpreting God's ways to man, he is a poet of facts, of concrete persons and things and events, in the selection, ordering, and expression of which the general significance of his themes becomes apparent. It is when he makes his generalisations explicit, instead of leaving them implicit, that his genius seems to desert him. One is tempted to suppose, however illegitimately, that some curious distrust of his own powers has urged him to his gravest errors, making him pile horrors on a main tragedy till its original force is obscured, or expatiate sentimentally on a situation which, dryly stated, is more moving than any comment on it could ever be. In *Pompey the Great*, a very faulty play, but one the tragedy of which is inherent in the action, after Pompey has been treacherously

118

murdered, the seaman on the Greek ship which has
carried him to Egypt haul on the sheets to the
accompaniment of a chanty conceived in the
following terms:—

THE CHANTY
" Kneel to the beautiful women who bear us this
strange brave fruit."

CHORUS
" Away, i-oh."

THE CHANTY
" Man with his soul so noble: man half god and
half brute."

CHORUS
" So away, i-oh."

This in spite of its form, in spite of the fact that
this galley of the first century before Christ carries
a " Bosun " and an officer who is addressed as
" Mr. Mate," is clearly not intended for a piece
of realism.   It is the author frankly endeavouring
to transcend his own setting in order to appear from
without as a moralist on the action—because, one
cannot help thinking, he does not trust the action
to speak for itself.   Compare with this two lines
from the last conversation in the condemned cell
between Jimmy Gurney and his mother.   (Jimmy,
it will be remembered, was, before he killed his
man, a navvy on the railway):—

" ' I s'pose they've brought the line beyond the
Knapp ? "
" ' Ay, and beyond the Barcle, so they say.' "

Nothing could be barer, nothing, in the context, could be more moving. A long passage of reflection could never bring home to the reader, as this does, the inarticulate agony of the condemned man and his widowed mother. It is simply a statement of fact; but a statement so contrived that all the comment that is necessary is, as it were, resonant in its overtones.

Mr. Masefield is pre-eminently the poet of fact. His power lies in invention, and it is thus, rather than directly, that he conveys the reflections which occur to him. It is when he does otherwise that he spoils his own achievement, by an additional irrelevant turn of the screw or by a moralising passage less impressive than the moral the reader has already drawn. Thus, in *Captain Margaret*, a book with some beautiful pages, he attempts to increase the hero's tragedy by exaggerating the wickedness of the villain and by making the heroine so stupid that one cries out against her as impossible or worthless. Thus in *Multitude and Solitude*, after Roger Naldrett's play has been ignominiously hissed off the stage, he spends a night so full of minor discomforts that the first effect is lost and passion degenerates into fretfulness. Thus, in a hundred vague and inconclusive lyrics and sonnets, Mr. Masefield reiterates the abstract noun "Beauty," proclaiming that " Beauty " is his faith and principle of movement:—

> " Beauty across the darkness hurled,
> Be it through me you shame the world "

—but never once providing the reader with any definite impression of what he means by that comprehensive word. Yet, by reference to those

120

of his writings in which it does not appear, one can discover easily enough what he means by it. There is beauty in the faith and love of Jimmy's mother; there is beauty in the courage which sends the Dauber, weakest and most timid of the crew, first on deck to go aloft in the storm when the ship is rounding Cape Horn; there is beauty in Nan's trusting surrender to Dick Gurvil. These are the things which make Mr. Masefield's faith and the substance of his poetry; but they are convincing only when he shows them, never when he talks about them.

It is because he is a genuine poet, with a besetting and genuinely dangerous temptation, that none of his work is perfect, much of it seriously flawed and little of it quite negligible. The attempt to distinguish throughout between the passages in which he has written naturally and those in which he has written counter to his own gifts would require a long book and would make, perhaps, a very tedious book. It might show how in *Good Friday* the deadly quietness and matter-of-factness of the opening create an impressive atmosphere which is afterwards dispelled by the introduction of a symbolic and generalising madman. It might show that it would be appropriate for Kurano, in *The Faithful*, to feign madness did not his oracular responses imitate too faithfully all the wise lunatics in Shakespeare. A differentiating catalogue in this style might possibly be useful, but would certainly be hard reading. It will be more to the point in this brief inquiry to discover if we can the work in which Mr. Masefield's virtues are most prominent and his faults least conspicuous.

There can be little doubt that this is to be found in *Reynard the Fox*, his last book but one, his longest, and, as I think, his most nearly perfect poem. It suffers a little, but almost negligibly, from the piling on of the horror, in that the fox has extraordinarily bad luck in the way of stopped earths; but setting this aside, together with minor blemishes of diction and rhyme, it is tolerably free from sentimentality or ill-judged moralisings. We might have had a fox that symbolised Beauty, or a fox that ran to pluck Beauty out of the heart of peril, or a disquisition on the unjust sufferings of the fox and their brutalising effects on the hunt. But here the poet avoids symbolism, and, for the rest, he is wisely impartial. He sees the hunt, the effort of the fox, and the exhilaration of the pursuers vividly and objectively. He accepts the fact and in all aspects of it he lays beauty bare. It is for him a spectacle, and the spectacle, as he conveys it, has a meaning; but he does not spoil our appreciation of the meaning by calling attention to it with a capital letter. Here, for once, he has observed a reasonable degree of reticence, trusting to the picture which he sees to awaken in others the emotion it has awakened in him—an emotion which is at once clear and definable, united and various. It is true that he is still over-anxious about the effect of his work. He does now and again force the pace, force the emotion, underline where it is not necessary, and he comes once or twice very close to the maudlin. But these faults are less frequent, and less destructive, than elsewhere in his work.

This poem has been called " Chaucerian "; and the opening pages are not unworthy of that majestic epithet. The persons are no doubt less vivid, less definite than those of the Prologue to the *Canterbury Tales*; their outlines are not so sharp,

their colours are paler. But the gusto with which
their characteristics are presented has in it something of Chaucer's relish of the difference in human
nature, from old Steven, who—

> " Shone on people like the sun
> And on himself for shining so,"

to

> " Bill, that big-mouthed smiler,
> They nick-named him the mug-beguiler."

and Sal Ridden:—

> " A loud, bold, blonde, abundant mare,
> With white horse-teeth and stooks of hair
> (Like polished brass), and such a manner
> It flaunted from her like a banner."

And a dozen more, as accurately and tersely drawn,
characteristic of time and place and not uncharac-
teristic of the people from which they spring.

It is in the joy in real things, in people, places
and events, that Mr. Masefield's power lies; and
he has never expressed this better than in *Reynard*,
in such passages as the description of the hounds
moving off:—

> " Round the corner came the Hunt,
> Those feathery things, the hounds, in front,
> Intent, wise, dipping, trotting, straying,
> Smiling at people, shoving, playing,
> Nosing to children's faces, waving
> Their feathery sterns, and all behaving,
> One eye to Dansey on Maroon,
> Their padding cat-feet beat a tune."

123

This is the thing itself; but no mere description, however exact, can convey, as this does, the spectator's delight in the thing. The whole poem is like this, a description that is something more; and, so far as it goes, it conveys a vision and an appreciation of a whole way of life and of the qualities and characteristics which emerge from it. What is to be found here without difficulty is equally present almost all through Mr. Masefield's work; but elsewhere it must be sought for and many hindrances in the way of finding it must be overcome and many disappointments must be endured. Nevertheless, Mr. Masefield's qualities are both real and rare; and the hindrances and disappointments make certainly a high, but, perhaps, not a prohibitive price to pay for them.

Mr. Belloc: Some Characteristics

ANY reader who has ever seen a full bibliography of Mr. Belloc's works will appreciate how hard a subject he is for critical treatment and why he has received so little of it. Many of his books are reprinted journalism, occasional essays first written to fill a set space in a daily paper. Many are purely controversial or informative in intention. He is a poet, a novelist, an economist, a historian, and a topographer. He has also a definite general attitude towards the world in which these various activities have their interrelated places: he is a philosopher. And hence even those works which are purely creative in form, his novels and poems and imaginative pictures of travel, never escape a tinge of tendenciousness. Similarly his controversial books are rarely without definite literary merit. And his journalism, though it is often hasty and careless, is not often empty and is not often without evidence of his creative power. In the number of varieties which his work presents he resembles Mr. Chesterton, with whom it is so usual to compare him. The comparison holds good also in the general attitude of both towards the world—an attitude which it is probably incorrect to say that Mr. Chesterton learnt from Mr. Belloc, the one having rather found in the other a confirmation of what he himself had already guessed. But beyond that point it breaks down. Mr. Chesterton has a firm grasp of a view of life, and is a poet and a fine rhetorician. His ideas are general and are best embodied by purely imaginative means, whereas his scholarship and command of detail are relatively small. He expresses himself most effectively in *The Napoleon of Notting Hill* and in passages of *The Ballad of the White Horse*—in stories and in poems. But when he comes to particulars he is as loose and vague as Mr. Belloc is firm and decided: he is a sage rather than a scientist, a rhapsodist rather than a debater. Mr. Belloc is also a poet and a rhetorician, but he does not support his general view of life only by poetry and rhetoric: he employs as well a firm handling, accurate or inaccurate, of facts.

He is therefore to some degree exempt from the modern dichotomy between literature as a means and literature as an end. Time was when many writers were able to take it for granted, without internal questionings, that serious literature ought to be used for practical and immediate purposes. Ibsen, Brieux, Tolstoi, all had done so. Mr. Wells confessed to Henry James that he would rather be called a journalist than an artist. Mr. Shaw used to feel dissatisfied with Shakespeare, because Shakespeare never wrote a play with the object of undoing a social abuse. Only the other day Mr. Shaw again, under the pressure of centenary celebrations, owned his willingness to accept Keats as a great poet—because *Isabella* is an attack on the capitalist system. But, though its first protagonists have not changed, this point of view is now no longer held to be unchallengeable. Observe the somewhat contemptuous implications contained in this recent remark of a not unintelligent critic: " The temptation, to any man who is interested in ideas and primarily in literature, to put literature into the corner until he has cleaned up the whole country first, is almost irresistible. Some persons, like Mr. Wells and Mr. Chesterton, have succeeded

so well in this latter profession of setting the house
in order, and have attracted so much more attention
than Arnold, that we must conclude that it is
indeed their proper rôle and that they have done
well for themselves in laying literature aside."
And if we conclude that they have laid literature
aside, then literature lays them aside; and we may
find ourselves, for the sake of a narrow and fanciful
definition, leaving them to a form of criticism which
is not competent, and does not attempt, to judge
them as writers.

This distinction, which is really unsafe when it
is so made as to convey in itself and by itself some
shade of regret or blame, has its uses. We may
regret that Mr. Wells writes nowadays *The Salvaging
of Civilisation* instead of another *Invisible Man*—
because *The Salvaging of Civilisation* is a badly
and hastily written and impermanent book. We
may blame Mr. Chesterton for scamping his poems
and stories so as to have time for attacking the
divorce laws or the party system or some other
bugbear—because thus he is deserting what he
can do well for something he does not so well.
But with Mr. Belloc the question does not present
itself in quite the same form.

He, whose most constant trait it is to have an
answer for everything, would probably not hesitate
to offer an opinion on this question, and would
most likely find any hard-and-fast distinction
between literature as a means and literature as an
end almost meaningless. He sees himself before
all else as a member of human society and in
particular as a member of a society which he believes
to be diseased. Moreover, he believes that he
knows the cure for this disease. His opinions
inevitably colour, not only in general spirit but

also in details, everything he writes: he cannot compose a jolly occasional essay on cheeses without introducing his earnest confidence in the surviving power of the Roman Empire:—

" As Europe fades away under the African wound which Spain suffered or the Eastern barbarism of the Elbe, what happens to cheese ? It becomes very flat and similar. You can quote six cheeses perhaps which the public power of Christendom has founded outside the limits of its ancient Empire—but not more than six. I will quote you 253 between the Ebro and the Grampians, between Brindisi and the Irish Channel.
I do not write vainly. It is a profound thing."

What he himself has written on literature is not much in quantity nor is it always very good; but it is possible to find in it quite clearly the opinion that literature is a part of the life of the state, an expression, and, if all is well, a strengthening expression of the condition of society. Good art appears when the state is healthy, bad art when it is not—though it is not always clear which way the deduction is drawn. In one place he tells us that the Barbarian is already upon us from within; and he draws his instances from the modern attitude towards marriage, property, mathematics, and painting. His comment on the poems of Hérédia is characteristic:—

" Perhaps the truest generalisation that can be made with regard to the French people is to say that they especially in Western Europe (whose quality it is ever to transform itself but never to die) discover new springs of vitality after every

128

period of defeat and aridity which they are compelled to cross. Hérédia will prove in the near future a capital example of this power."

His own system is so complete and connected that it does not allow him to make water-tight divisions between its parts. The poet is for him no less a direct servant of the state than the political controversialist; and the poet need suffer no change of nature when he enters into political controversy. The choice between the career of the artist and the career of the publicist can never have had for him any reality. His belief that it is his duty to preach certain truths is so deep-seated as to be part of the temperament in which his poetry originates. His perception of these truths and their importance is an essential part of his perception of the world as a whole. A range of mountains or a river strikes him simultaneously under three aspects—physical beauty, historical association, political meaning.

I am not concerned here with the details or the absolute merits of Mr. Belloc's philosophy. It is an extraordinarily complete and consistent structure in which are reconciled the doctrines of the Catholic Church and of Rousseau, of the Christian religion, and of modern democracy as the French Revolution made it. This structure is maintained by a belief in the gradual, not catastrophic, development of Europe and Christendom out of the Roman Empire, a belief derived from that great, still almost unknown master, Fustel de Coulanges. His reading of English history, with its insistence on the aristocratic and increasingly oligarchic nature of our constitution, was largely anticipated by Disraeli. The philosophers whom he most trusts are St. Thomas Aquinas and Rousseau; and both are philosophers of certitude. St. Thomas recognises dogma and Rousseau establishes it for himself. No doubt Mr. Belloc's own system of fact and thought owes much of its influence to its definiteness and consistency. In a world of half doubts and provisional certainties it stands inflexible, sincere, and, if limited, complete. Other systems, whether that of Mr. Shaw or that of Mr. Wells, whatever their novelty and their speculative interest, are less stable as a framework by which men can live, and are besides necessarily incomplete. And Mr. Belloc's importance as a man of evident intelligence and knowledge believing, at a time when other men of intelligence and knowledge doubted, can hardly be rated too high. Belief often may be misplaced; but it is always, of itself, more attractive than doubt to the majority of mankind. Mr. Belloc has been able to prove that this is really true also of many of the cultured minority. He brought to the educated few, in their own language, some of the certitudes of the uneducated many. He made known the reasons for holding a faith which is most commonly held without reasons; and the force of his example has been very great. He might be called the apostle to the intellectuals. It is possible to criticise his attitude in many ways. You may regard him as the reactionary last defender of a vanishing creed or as the first sign of a restoration. But, however it be interpreted, his influence is a real thing. And it is the influence exercised by a writer who brings to the help of his proselytising zeal great literary skill and much poetic force.

Mr. Belloc: Some Characteristics

The characteristic by which Mr. Belloc is best known to the public at large is his humour. Possibly since 1914 his deepest impression on the popular mind has been made as an exponent of military matters. But before that date the one echo which the mention of his name was sure to provoke was the title of one of his earliest books, *The Bad Child's Book of Beasts*. These verses were unmixed with satire or controversy; and he does not always harness his humour to a purpose. But very often his humour is that of the controversialist. A man who throws himself so wholeheartedly into his own argument cannot but find something absurd in those who oppose him; and when he is at his most earnest, his scornful, aggressive and triumphant laughter is apt to break out. It is then at once a weapon of offence and an expression of his certainty in his own opinion:—

> " We also know the sacred height
>   Up on Tugela side,
> Where those three hundred fought with Beit
>   And fair young Wernher died.
>
> . . . The little empty homes forlorn,
> The ruined synagogues that mourn,
>   In Frankfort and Berlin;
> We knew them when the peace was torn—
> We of a nobler lineage born—
> And now by all the gods of scorn
>   We mean to rub them in."

The gods of scorn have been powerful gods on

Mr. Belloc's side; and he is never behindhand in invoking their help.

His series of political novels is the place in which, apart from a few verses, he has most exercised his gift of satire. These books are not all quite the same in character, nor are they equal in merit. *Emmanuel Burden*, the earliest of them, is curiously uneven and straggling in construction; and its unevenness largely springs from the fact that here more often and more noticeably than elsewhere the author allows a graver tone, whether of anger or of pity, to come through the satire. In such passages, excellent as they are, the ironic assumption of partisanship with the villains becomes too thin and formal a veil over the real intention. Emmanuel Burden is a London merchant of the older, Victorian type, who allows himself to be led away by financiers of the modern school. These, according to Mr. Belloc, are ruining England; and at last Burden's own happiness is ruined by them. In this book we find the first appearance of Mr. Barnett, who afterwards becomes Lord Lambeth and then Duke of Battersea; and nowhere else (except perhaps in one passage in *Pongo and the Bull*) does Mr. Belloc speak of Mr. Barnett, who for him personifies the enemy, with quite so much hostility and loathing. He quite obviously hates Mr. Barnett and Mr. Harbury and Major Pondo and all the other persons concerned in the adventure of the M'Korio Delta Development Co. As obviously, he is moved by the fate of Mr. Burden, who is literally killed by the realisation that his commercial enterprises have made him a party to an underhand attack on his oldest friend. The account of his last journey home, after this realisation, is one of the most affecting things that Mr. Belloc has ever

132

written, and is no less serious because its tone is
sometimes ironical and cynical:—

" In the train he sat, relieved by some repose,
and conscious (in a blurred way) that an old man
in the corner of a railway carriage was safer from
insult and observation, than wandering on a plat-
form, a thing for gibes.

" He sat dully, his brows contracting now and
then. The names of the stations pleased him,
because they were familiar. He tried to remember
their order, or at least the name of such as he had
not yet reached; but he could not. He was puzzled,
and looked round at his fellow-passengers, as
though for help. They glanced at him above their
papers, and saw that he was ill. They feared for
the decencies. One, more refined than the rest,
bolted out at the next stopping-place. The others
defended themselves with silence, reading steady
behind the bulwark of the evening papers.

". . . Then there was a little darkness and a
rumble, and he heard the name of Norwood. He
recognised it at once, and got out, and stood
irresolutely at the gate. The collector took the
ticket out of his hand, and smiled. Mr. Burden
looked at him fixedly, wondering at his smile, and
felt for a moment an angry wave of emotion. He
took this man also for one of his enemies.

" But a muddled feeling of pleasant association
came after. He took him foolishly for a friend,
and smiled and nodded in reply. Then, by pure
instinct, such as animals have, he found the way
towards his home.

" He came up that familiar road, his head reeling,
and a bond, as though of iron, oppressing it within;
and, as he walked, he suffered some dull ache

continually. His slow steps jarred him; and now and then those pulsating throbs that are Death's artillery preparing his attack, hammered at the walls of his being."

But there will be no more tragedies in Mr. Belloc's political novels and no characters, except detached observers, with whom the reader is asked to sympathise. Mr. Clutterbuck, although he loses his seat, will get his knighthood, George Mulross Demaine will get his appointment as Warden of the Court of Dowry; and though an elderly Leader of the Opposition is chased by a savage bull till " the sweat of fifty years stood or rather leapt across the deathly face of the agonised man," this is an incident presented for laughter, not for pity. Nevertheless, the argument begun in the first novel is continued in those which succeed it. English politics have been corrupted. They are determined by inane or dishonest politicians and obscenely unscrupulous financiers. The rich are abnormal or wicked, or both. Only now Mr. Belloc substitutes untroubled and even more hearty laughter for the rather bitter laughter of *Emmanuel Burden* in which he mingled both anger and pity. The tone of these later books is summarised in the admirable figure of Mr. William Bailey. It was Mr. Bailey's hobby to compile a dictionary of Jews who had changed their names; but he did this without bitterness, and he found occasion for uninterrupted amusement in the vagaries and degradations of the society to which he himself belonged.

This concentration on politics and finance, and on a particular view of them, might well become monotonous. It does indeed begin to do so in

Pongo and the Bull and *The Green Overcoat*, where
the humour is less abundant and exuberant, more
strained and mechanical, than in their predecessors.
But at its best, Mr. Belloc's humour, whether used
for a purpose or for its own sake, is marked by an
extraordinary gusto for detail and a great richness of comic invention. The first of these qualities
may be exemplified (at random) by the account in
Emmanuel Burden of the porter employed by the
M'Korio Delta Development Co.:—

" This man was a Swedish Protestant; in height
he was fully six feet seven, his hair was of the colour
of tow, his eyes were of a faded blue, his face was
white and yellow; in intellect, while not deficient,
he was of a deliberation which admirably suited
the nature of his employment; nor could any
length of hours passed in the public gaze at the
Main Entrance weary the Northern steadfastness
of his mind. . . . I would I had the space or
leisure to deal at further length with this remarkable
and simple figure; indeed, long before Mr. Burden's
death, it was my intention to devote to the portrayal
of this porter's life and character that literary skill
which has now been turned into another, a far
graver, and I fear more monotonous channel. I
had intended to relate exactly his career. How,
stranded in the docks of London, this towering
Scandinavian had obtained employment as a Life-
guard; how, deserting from his Corps on account
of the bullying to which he was subjected by his
comrades, he found his way into the Metropolitan
Police. Dismissed from this force for drunkenness,
he became a chucker-out in a Music Hall, in which
post his grievous muscular weakness, universal in
men of his type, soon proved him unfit to deal

with that athletic youth which frequents such
haunts in the hey-day of its vigour; how, finally,
while posing as a Giant in a Fair, a position he
occupied in return for his bare food, he was tempted
to break his contract at the prospect of a higher
wage. At the persuasion of Mr. Barnett himself,
he fled by night, accepted the service and livery
of the M'Korio, and so reached the culmination
of his career."

This portrait, so exact in its details, so absurd in
its place and in its gravity, is a sign of the natural
exuberance where Mr. Belloc's comic invention has
its roots. And this natural exuberance naturally
takes its way into absurdities, into sudden unexpected
turns of phrase and brusque ruptures of the expected
relations of things. In the breathless, helter-skelter
farce of *A Change in the Cabinet*, where Mr. Belloc
is undoubtedly expressing his opinions, he invents
for his politicians and financiers an uproarious
series of incidents; and these are conceived in
such high spirits that one can, if one wishes, forget
the purpose in which they were begun. There is
no better story in all his novels than that of the
feeble-minded Demaine, who, on the eve of his
appointment to the Cabinet, is whisked away into
an astonishing and ignominious sequence of mari-
time adventures, and returns, strangely clad, to
read solemnly to the delighted Prime Minister a
narrative of peril on the high seas specially composed
for him by Mr. William Bailey. In *The Path to
Rome*, where he is not expressing opinions but
disporting in light-hearted buffoonery on the Ending
of Books, he puts a grotesque close to his disquisition
by the expression of a political dislike: "Homer
ends with lines that might as well be in the middle

136

of a passage; Hesiod, I know not how; and Mr.
Bailey, the New Voice from Eurasia, does not end
at all, but is still going on."

Thus poetry and opinion are mixed in his work,
because he himself makes no distinction between
them: it is the natural characteristic of exuberance
not to be influenced by such distinctions. The
last-named book, perhaps his best known after
The Bad Child's Book of Beasts, certainly does not
set out to argue any thesis, and yet most of the
author's deepest beliefs might be deduced from its
pages. It is the narrative of a journey in a direct
line from Toul to Rome; and because to Mr.
Belloc all things are interconnected the intervening
landscape draws from him by the way of an expression of all his opinions, from his belief in the
efficacy of the Mass—" The most important cause
of this feeling of satisfaction is that you are doing
what the human race has done for thousands upon
thousands upon thousands of years "—to his belief
in the fundamental difference between the Latin
and Teutonic races. And because of his innate
expansiveness and energy he supplements the
narrative with anecdotes, stories, and incidental
absurdities, and one or two very good verses.
One of the stories may be quoted, for it has a second
interest besides being good fun. The Padre
Eterno is sitting in Heaven, with St. Michael
beside him, and asks what is a certain spot of
light shining far away in the void. When St.
Michael, a little offended, has explained that it is
the Earth, the Padre Eterno asks:—

" ' . . . Michael, what are those little things
swarming up and down all over it ? '

" ' Those,' said St. Michael, ' are Men.'

" ' I really beg your pardon,' said the Padre Eterno, when he saw the importance attached to these little creatures. " I am sure they are worthy of the very fullest attention, and ' (he added, for he was sorry to have offended), ' how sensible they seem, Michael! There they go, buying and selling, and sailing, driving, and wiving, and riding, and dancing, and singing, and the rest of it; indeed, they are most practical, business-like, and satisfactory little beings. But I notice one odd thing. Here and there are some not doing as the rest, or attending to their business, but throwing themselves into all manner of attitudes, making the most extraordinary sounds, and clothing themselves in the quaintest of garments. What is the meaning of that ? '

" ' Sire! ' cried St. Michael, in a voice that shook the architraves of heaven, ' they are worshipping You! '

" ' Oh! they are worshipping *me*! Well, that is the most sensible thing I have heard of them yet, and I altogether commend them. *Continuez*,' said the Padre Eterno, ' *continuez !* ' And since then all has been well with the world; at least where *ils continuent*."

Here again, I think, we find another reason for the real force of Mr. Belloc's influence. His humour is robust: his religion is no less so, and presents itself as a thing hardy and tested enough to stand the ordinary strains of the world. The central qualities of his work are strength, exuberance, decision; and all these qualities manifest themselves in his humorous writings, to which they give their individual flavour and effect.

Mr. Belloc: Some Characteristics

There is a fourth quality in Mr. Belloc's work
which I have not yet mentioned. I mean its
lucidity; and it is this which makes him so effective
a controversialist. He does indeed lack some of
the arts of the preacher: he cannot, or will not,
persuade:—

" I say the Catholic ' conscience ' of History—I
say ' conscience '—that is, an intimate knowledge
through identity: the intuition of a thing which
is one with the Knower—I do not say ' The Catholic
Aspect of History.' This talk of ' aspects ' is
modern and therefore part of a decline: it is false,
and therefore ephemeral: I will not stoop to it. I
will rather do homage to truth and say that there
is no such thing as a Catholic ' aspect ' of European
history. There is a Protestant aspect, a Jewish
aspect, a Mohammedan aspect, a Japanese aspect,
and so forth. For all of these look on Europe from
without. The Catholic sees Europe from within.
There is no more a Catholic ' aspect ' of European
history than there is a man's ' aspect ' of himself.
. . . The Catholic brings to history (when I say
' history ' in these pages I mean the history of
Christendom) self-knowledge. As a man in the
confessional accuses himself of what he knows to
be true and what other people cannot judge, so a
Catholic, talking of the united European civilisation,
when he blames it, blames it for motives and for
acts which are his own. He himself could have
done these things in person. He is not relatively
right in his blame, he is absolutely right. As a
man can testify to his own motive, so can the

Catholic testify to unjust, irrelevant, or ignorant conceptions of the European story; for he knows why and how it proceeded."

This may or may not be true; but it is a sort of preaching which, if it be not addressed to the already converted, must be addressed to the easily intimidated. It is not so much advocacy as bullying. Nevertheless, it has obviously one of the prime virtues of all controversial writing. You may or may not like Mr. Belloc's meaning: you are at all events in no doubt as to what that meaning is.

Lucidity is a quality of style; and it seems proper in this place to insert among these notes a note upon the characteristics of Mr. Belloc's style. The fact of his French ancestry has been stated so often and has been made the basis of so many misunderstandings, that one hesitates to bring it out again. And yet in one thing at least, I think, it is apparent and of importance. It has been very well said that the reason for the superiority of the French prose-writers over our own, especially in prose which is not purely imaginative, is that while they have at their disposal a comparatively small number of words the meanings of all these words are exactly ascertained. Now in this respect Mr. Belloc's prose style is rather French than English. His vocabulary is not large, though it is by no means conventional. There are certain shades of expression which are definitely outside his range, certain things which he cannot successfully do. Even when one of his essays must be described as conversational in tone, it is the conversation of a man who has been warmed into something like oratory by his interest in his subject—Latin conversation rather than English. But what he does

140

say is always precise and comprehensible. Nor is it merely that his readers can be in no doubt as to what he means. The good effects of this natural lucidity begin to work at an earlier stage than that: he is never in doubt himself as to what he means.

It is apparent, like all his qualities, in its degree, throughout all his work. It contributed largely to the success of his commentary on military events, which, though, part rightly and part wrongly, it is not now rated so high as in 1914 and 1915, was probably the greatest feat of journalism accomplished by any single man during the War. It is always present, when all the other qualities of style have disappeared. Any reader who will look back at the extracts given in the earlier part of this essay and examine them closely will see that Mr. Belloc is not an author who writes prose for the sole purpose of creating beauty. He is often careless of the arrangement of words, of rhythm and harmony, of the balance of sentences and paragraphs. His work has been mostly journalism, very hastily written; and in the total number of his essays, somewhere between two and three hundred, very few could be described as perfect, though not many are quite negligible. But the strong flood of his knowledge and his opinions hardly ever abates; and wherever he is seeking to impart knowledge or enforce an opinion, whatever his haste, whatever his carelessness, he is careful to see that his meaning is plain.

I do not intend to suggest that there are not in his writings many beautiful passages which spring purely from the emotions and approximate to the condition of poetry. There are many such passages here and there in the essays, and one which is very good at the end of *The Four Men*. And, as always

141

in Mr. Belloc's work, it is exceedingly difficult to disentangle the single strand of verbal or poetic beauty—what he himself, speaking of Hérédia, calls the *beauté du verbe*—from the rest. If we take his travel-books alone, their appeal to us is mixed. We find in them beside the humour I have already described, both pictures of landscape, emotional in colour, and historical narrative and topographical detail, ostensibly at least purely informative. But who shall say how much the pictures of landscape attract us by their accuracy and precision, how much the history and the topography by the feeling which Mr. Belloc puts into them ? Here is a very characteristic passage from *Esto Perpetua*, describing the lateen-sail of the Mediterranean :—

" It is not of our own making, and, indeed, it bears a foreign mark which is very distinct, and which puzzles every northerner when first he comes across this sail: it reefs along the yard. Why it should do so neither history nor the men that handle it can explain, since single sails are manifestly made to reef from the foot to the leach, where a man can get at them. Not so the lateen. If you carry too much canvas and the wind is pressing her you must take it in from aloft, or, it may be supposed, lower the whole on deck. And this foreign, quaint, unusual thing which stamps the lateen everywhere is best seen when the sail is put away in harbour. It does not lie down along the deck as do ours in the north, but right up along the yard, and the yard itself is kept high at the masthead, making a great bow across the sky, and (one would say) tempting Providence to send a gale and wreck it.

". . . There is nothing makes a man's heart so buoyant as to see one of the little ships bowling along breast-high towards him, with the wind and the clouds behind it, careering over the sea. It seems to have borrowed something of the air and something of the water, and to unite them both and to be their offspring and also their bond. When they are middle-way over the sea towards one under a good breeze, the little ships are things to remember.

"So it is when they carry double sail and go, as we say of our schooners, 'wing and wing.' For they can carry two sails when the wind is moderate, and especially when the vessel is running before it, but these two sails are not carried upon two masts, but both upon the same mast. The one is the common or working sail, carried in all weathers. The other is a sort of spinnaker of which you may see the yard lying along decks in harbour or triced up a little by the halyard, so as to swing clear of the hands.

". . . Moreover the sails of these little ships never seem to lose the memory of power. Their curves and fulness always suggest a movement of the hull. Very often at sunset when the dead calm reflects things unbroken like an inland pond, the topmost angle of these lateens catches some hesitating air that stirs above, and leads it down the sail, so that a little ripple trembles round the bows of the boat, though all the water beside them is quite smooth, and you see her gliding in without oars. She comes along in front of the twilight, as gradual and as silent as the evening, and seems to be impelled by nothing more substantial than the advance of darkness."

There is in this a curious, yet natural, mingling

of the poetical and the practical. It conveys the emotions aroused by the sight of these ships: it contains also sound information about them, obviously noted by an observer with some knowledge of boat-sailing. Compare it with the passage I have quoted above from *Europe and the Faith*, and you will see that, dissimilar as they are in subject and purpose, they have the same lucidity. And this quality, one which is admirable in itself (though perhaps a certain price must be paid for it), unites all Mr. Belloc's work and provides something which *The Servile State* and his most frivolous piece of fooling have in common.

IV

Possibly in time the greater part of Mr. Belloc's prose, tendencious as so much of it is, hasty and careless as nearly all of it is, may disappear. Even if it does so, the historical fact of his influence will remain and, I think, will not be forgotten; but it will then be a matter of social history rather than of literature. And his poetry is so small in extent, so unambitious in appearance, that one might be forgiven for thinking it inadequate to preserve in future times the memory of one who bulked so large in his own. Yet his verse is in some ways himself in epitome. Most even of his opinions can be found in it, and all his qualities—without some of the defects which circumstances have engendered in his prose.

It is, of course, the usual mixture—Mr. Belloc's objections to genres being apparently insuperable. He is, as every one knows, one of the most dexterous of light versifiers. *The Bad Child's Book of Beasts*,

Mr. Belloc: Some Characteristics

More Peers, and *The Modern Traveller* are classics
with an independent standing. These verses are
a little in that vein:—

> " The Freshman ambles down the High,
>   In love with everything he sees,
> He notes the very Midland sky,
>   He sniffs a more than Midland breeze.
>
> ' Can this be Oxford ? This the place ? '
>   (He cries) " of which my father said
> The tutoring was a damned disgrace,
>   The creed a mummery, stuffed and dead ?
>
> . . . Is it from here the people come,
>   Who talk so loud and roll their eyes,
> And stammer ? How extremely rum!
>   How curious! What a great surprise."

The poem continues, and we come to this:—

> " I will not try the reach again,
>   I will not set my sail alone,
> To moor a boat bereft of men
>   At Yarnton's tiny docks of stone.
>
> But I will sit beside the fire,
>   And put my hand before my eyes,
> And trace, to fill my heart's desire,
>   The last of all our Odysseys.
>
> The quiet evening kept her tryst:
>   Beneath an open sky we rode,
> And passed into a wandering mist
>   Along the perfect Evenlode,

The tender Evenlode that makes
   Her meadows hush to hear the sound
Of waters mingling in the brakes,
   And binds my heart to English ground.

A lovely river, all alone,
   She lingers in the hills and holds
A hundred little towns of stone,
   Forgotten in the western wolds.

He is the least obviously ambitious of poets; but his work in verse has the rocklike permanence of the sonnets of Hérédia whom he so much admires. He has not, it is true, any closer affinities with the French writer. His range is wider, his style is more flexible: his poems are executed in flesh, not in stone. But they themselves, their subjects and their phrases, give the same impression of scrupulous, unremittingly careful, *choice*. He seems to revolve a theme for many years before he clothes it in the quietly and beautifully appropriate language which is its only proper dress. His small production includes epigrams and little satires, carols and drinking-songs, ballads and sonnets and chanties. Not all of these are equally good. But they are all clearly written with much greater general care, with much more attention to the *beauté du verbe*, than his prose; and the best of them have a curious soundness of texture and a fullness of flavour that make his distinguishing qualities. And it is impressive to see how little he has written, considering the great outpouring of his prose. With most poets a small output, whatever else it may suggest, does not as a rule indicate great energy or great reserves of power. We know, however, that Mr. Belloc is not deficient in energy, that the small

146

volume of his verse cannot be a sign of flaccidness. It is explained by its own excellence. It is, as it were, the outlet of the artist in him, that artist who in prose has been submerged by considerations which to the rational man seemed more important.

And while the rational man has given himself, could not but give himself, to immediate work at immediate problems, the poet has expressed the fundamental ideas which underlie that philosophy of life. Mr. Belloc's poems do not lie aside from the rest of his work. They express his religion, his love of home, his love of friends, his love of " a good time "; and these are as essential to his philosophy as any views he may hold on politics or economics. And, in spite of their unambitious appearance, they will serve as an enduring representation of his work. It would indeed have been strange if a writer whose fantasies teach history and whose histories are as entertaining as novels had written poems which did anything less.

The Work of Mr. H. G. Wells

THE paragraphists and gossipers, who know such things, tell us that Mr. Wells is unable to speak in public. But perhaps the power of oratory is withering in the modern world. There are too many people. The busiest politician cannot make on more than a small proportion of those whom he would influence that direct and personal impact which was made by Gladstone and Mr. Bryan on subjugated and devoted audiences. A few thousands at most can gather within range of the speaker's voice: the rest of the nation must be reached through the medium of print. The speeches of Senator Hughes and M. Briand at the Washington Conference, which produced so deep an effect throughout the world, were conceived and delivered as oratory; but they came to an overwhelming proportion of the minds they were meant to influence in the shape of newspaper articles. And simultaneously Mr. Wells also was in Washington addressing the same audience in the same manner.

The importance of the direct personal impact must not even now be underrated. It cannot make a nation of enthusiasts; but it can leaven a nation with enthusiasts. Nevertheless, its importance is diminishing. The orator, with his physical gifts, is being reduced nearly to an equality with the publicist who may have none. The publicist grows in importance. When Mr. Wells went to Washington to comment on the proceedings there we were informed that no journalist had ever before addressed so large an audience; and this was very likely true. If we gave less deep and immediate attention to his articles than to the speeches of Senator Hughes and M. Briand, it was only because the utterances of statesmen are thought to be not merely persuasive but also revealing. It is possible that M. Briand will betray what the rulers of the world intend to do: Mr. Wells cannot, because he is not one of them. But, this aside, Mr. Wells's letters from Washington, not merely commenting but urging a policy with every art of persuasion, form the modern counterpart, if only in embryo, of the oratorical " campaigns " which in England, and especially in America, made so conspicuous a part of political life during the last century.

Especially in America. These words are not without significance: for if Mr. Wells in his capacity as publicist is to be compared with the tribe of orators, then the comparison is closest with a type of orator which is rather American than English. He is a spell-binder, a silver-tongue. Though he conveys it only through the written word, he relies much on personality and a known personality. He uses the silver-tongue's devices of humour and especially humorous confession; he makes elementary facts and almost platitudinous principles appear vivid and concrete and new; he rises, without putting a distance between himself and his audience, into passages of emotional eloquence. The style of his later books does closely resemble that of modern oratory—not the oratory of Gladstone even, still less that of Burke or Grattan, but perhaps that of Mr. Lloyd George.

Especially in America. Or perhaps we might equally well substitute for that word the phrase,

" a new country." Some one remarked in the
early days of the war, when Mr. Wells was killing
invaders with his rook-rifle and winding up all the
armament firms in the world, that he had about
him something reminiscent of a Colonial Premier.
He has all the advantages and disadvantages of
being detached from the enormous weight of
tradition which is the common appendage of
European thinkers. He proceeds to settle whatever problem may be before him without suspecting
that it may have its roots in something outside his
horizon—though that horizon is continually expanding. Some curious accident has done for him
what the Atlantic has done for American statesmen.
It has severed an umbilical cord: the facts and the
meaning of the vast, tumbled, contradictory record
of European development are things foreign to
him—things which can be learnt indeed but which
have not with him, as with most writers born and
educated in Europe, early and natural roots in the
mind. There are American statesmen who seem
to believe that such world-history as need be known
began with President Monro or President Lincoln.
Mr. Wells, for a great part of his life (perhaps even
now, save in so far as he finds there a source of
horrible examples), has believed that it begins—
when ? with his birth ? with the initiation of his
scientific studies ? or perhaps with the moment
when Mr. and Mrs. Sidney Webb " appeared
riding very rapidly upon bicycles from the direction
of London " and urged him " to ioin and stimulate
the Fabians ? "

It might be possible by guessing to hit on some explanation of the " accident " of which I spoke above. Mr. Wells's education, it is legitimate to deduce from several of his books, was grotesquely inefficient until it became exclusively scientific. And he was a science-student in a decade when the worship of science, the conception of it as a pre-eminent and all-sufficing form of learning, was perhaps at its height. Add to this the odd fact that in him immense literary ability somehow exists without the literary turn of mind. He is of all good writers the least a man of letters, and it is minds of a literary turn which most naturally and unconsciously absorb tradition and make it a part of themselves. Mr. Wells insisted in his controversy with Henry James that he was a journalist: he was not, he was not, an artist! And yet he has been, and sometimes still is, an artist in spite of himself.

Although he had written *The Wheels of Chance* and *Love and Mr. Lewisham*—not inconspicuous books—he was known, until he published *Kipps* in 1905, almost entirely, both to the general and to the more carefully selective public, as a writer of scientific romances. His first novel, *The Time Machine*, set the key: it was followed by a series of similar improbabilities ingeniously made probable. His gifts of plausibility and invention were indeed so great that they obscured all other qualities and got for him that very misleading title of " the English Jules Verne." Jules Verne shall never be lightly spoken of by me; but even if one looks no further than plausibility and invention the

comparison is unfair to the English writer. Jules
Verne wrote for boyish, eager and uncritical readers,
with a robust and hearty disregard for detail. Mr.
Wells could imagine as daringly; but his romances
will stand adult scrutiny and their detail is fashioned
with great care.

Put side by side Jules Verne's airship in *The
Clipper of the Clouds* and the mechanical devices
which Mr. Wells invents for his Martians. In
the first case the existence of the machine is asserted
and the reader must make a round, thumping act
of faith before going further into the story. But
the Martians' fighting-machines and handling-
machines are visualised, are made to work before
our eyes with touches of description and explanation
(and confession of ignorance) so cunningly applied
that, for so long as we are reading, the difficulty
of believing in them is almost negligible. Mr.
Wells never had a contrivance harder to describe
than his Time Machine, and this is how he
does it:—

"'This little affair,' said the Time Traveller,
resting his elbows upon the table and pressing his
hands together above the apparatus, 'is only a
model. It's my plan for a machine to travel through
time. You will notice that it looks singularly
askew, and that there is an odd twinkling appearance
about this bar, as though it was in some way
unreal.' He pointed to the part with his finger.
'Also, here is one little white lever, and here is
another.'

"The Medical Man got out of his chair and
peered into the thing. 'It's beautifully made,'
he said.

"'. . . Would you like to see the Time Machine

itself?' asked the Time Traveller. And therewith, taking the lamp in his hand, he led the way down the long, draughty corridor to his laboratory. I remember vividly the flickering light, his queer, broad head in silhouette, the dance of the shadows, how we all followed him, puzzled but incredulous, and how there in the laboratory we beheld a larger edition of the little mechanism we had seen vanish from before our eyes. Parts were of nickel, parts of ivory, parts had certainly been filed or sawn out of rock crystal. The thing was generally incomplete, but the twisted crystalline bars lay unfinished upon the bench beside some sheets of drawings, and I took one up for a better look at it. Quartz it seemed to be."

This is sleight of hand, it is almost charlatanry; but it is amazingly well done. The surroundings, the incidentals, are made as vivid and real as possible, while nothing definite is said of the object which is really the centre of the picture. A machine to travel through time might very well look like any other machine; but if it were so described we should probably be less ready to believe in its marvellous powers. Mr. Wells gives one or two meaningless details, and our imagination fills in the gap quite solidly enough for the purposes of the story. A caricaturist was once asked by a sitter to be merciful to a very prominent nose. He accordingly omitted the nose altogether, leaving a blank in the line of the profile; and the nose spread out into the margin of the picture indefinitely huge. Mr. Wells's device is the same. He has the first necessary quality of a literary artist: he knows what to leave out.

I could multiply examples of this ingenuity; and

indeed they are interesting to contemplate. In most of his books, it is true, Mr. Wells is working on a sounder scientific basis than in *The Time Machine*. In *The Invisible Man* there is not so much for him to slide over. There are two direct assertions. Griffin finds a way to bleach the living blood. He also discovers how to reduce the refractive index of the substances of the living body to an equality with that of air. We find no difficulty in believing that these discoveries *might* be made; and such a belief is all that the story requires. The author's skill consists in making their attainment and results seem lifelike. So it is in *The Food of the Gods*, where Redwood and Bensington first discover that growth is caused by the intermittent presence of a hitherto unknown substance in the blood, and then produce this substance artificially, enabling growth to become continuous. So in *The First Men in the Moon*, where Cavor makes a shield which is opaque to the rays of gravitation. There is nothing flimsy in the dexterity with which these openings are contrived. Mr. Wells uses a purely artistic strictness in concentrating all his powers, in the first chapters of these stories, on inducing in the reader the attitude of belief necessary for what follows.

Two qualities are to be observed in the developments which succeed these openings; and they are qualities for lack of which most scientific romances go to shipwreck. One is their severe and logical inevitability. Mr. Wells never makes his story easier to handle by neglecting any of the necessary consequences of the original thesis: he uses the consequences as material. An ordinary imagination would probably be content with the adventures which invisibility would make possible to the possessor of it, and would find it convenient to ignore the disadvantages. Mr. Wells makes his story out of the disadvantages. The second is the strong but controlled flow of living detail in which his stories are clothed. They are not, as ordinary imaginations would make them, merely ingenious. If one thinks of the Invisible Man, one does not think of a figure whose only characteristic is that he is invisible: one thinks of Griffin, egotistic, brutal, monomaniac. The ingenious idea is worked out to its last ramification in terms of character and the reactions of character. Mr. Wells has thus raised the scientifically fantastic romance, generally so poor or so crude a thing, to a serious level in the art of story-telling, to a level which it has never reached before.

And these devices and qualities are those of the natural teller of stories. In his introduction to *The Country of the Blind*, Mr. Wells wrote of the short story:—

" So that it is moving and delightful, it does not matter whether it is as ' trivial ' as a Japanese print of insects seen closely between grass stems, or as spacious as the prospect of the plain of Italy from Monte Mottarone. It does not matter whether it is human or inhuman, or whether it leaves you thinking deeply or radiantly but superficially pleased."

So Scheherazade might have spoken, if she had rationalised on her methods of survival; but not so the writer who really considers literature as a means rather than as an end and who would rather be called a journalist than an artist. These phrases, however, taken from the celebrated dispute with Henry James, are only examples of his curious

impulsiveness in controversy. He does not mean
what he says.

Some of his stories do indeed " leave you
thinking deeply "; but it is not because they are
acute journalism. I shall return to these. Most of
them are simply " inventions," scientific or other,
made real for a moment by the writer's skill purely
for the reader's entertainment. They are exposi-
tions of what Mr. Wells calls " the jolly art of
making something very bright and moving."
Many of them do not even depend on character
or emotion for their interest: these elements are
introduced only as aids to verisimilitude. *Æpyornis
Island* is the tale of a man who hatches out the egg
of an extinct bird on a desert island and finds it
inconveniently large and fierce—" I told him straight
that I didn't mean to be chased about a desert
island by any damned anachronisms." *The Stolen
Bacillus* is a tale of an Anarchist who stole a tube
of germs from a bacteriologist and departed to
poison the water-supply of London: when he was
pursued he drank the contents. " And I wanted
to astonish him, not knowing he was an Anarchist,
and took up a cultivation of that new species of
Bacterium I was telling you of that infest, and I
think cause, the blue patches upon various monkeys;
and, like a fool, I said it was Asiatic cholera."
These stories are of precisely the same character
as those which make up the Arabian Nights:
they are told with the purpose of giving entertainment. In this particular branch of literature
I do not think that any English writer, except Mr.
Kipling, and, in a lesser degree, Stevenson, has ever
been so successful as Mr. Wells. It is, one might
add, an art which seems almost to have disappeared.

The writing of short stories is an effective

schooling in the technique of construction. A well-constructed story is, quite simply, one which pins the reader's interest and makes itself easy, to the measure of its theme, for him to grasp. No failure here is forgiven to the man who attempts narrative; and Mr. Wells rarely fails. His short stories are compact, symmetrical and economically written. So, too, are his longer romances. *The Invisible Man* and *The War of the Worlds* are admirably built up so as to present and exhaust their themes, without overloading. *The War in the Air*, later than these and already propagandist, is a remarkable example of technical skill. The subject is a war in which all the world joins, and in which civilisation is smashed to pieces. The author's problem is to show how this happens, how it affects the world and how it affects individuals. He chooses as his eye-piece Bert Smallways, a smart limited Cockney mechanic, who is caught up by a series of amusing chances into the German air-fleet, sees its destruction of New York and its own destruction by the Asiatic forces, makes his way back to England, founds what he calls a " Viligance Committee " in a village there and settles down to keep pigs among the ruins. Now and again Mr. Wells, generally by the device of explaining something seen but not understood by Bert, takes a wider view, and in a sort of panorama, always without effort or irrelevancy, sketches in the world-wide background of disaster and confusion. In the perfect tact of these alternations of method this book reaches an extraordinarily high level of efficiency in construction. How well it treats its subject may be seen by comparing it with *The World Set Free*, a later book of similar purpose, rather more ambition and much less success. Here there is no continuous thread like the adventures of Bert Smallways. There is a series of disconnected episodes centring round unconnected characters; and the book moves from one to another and into long passages of quasi-historical summary with an effect of confusing incoherence.

III

The word " artist," as I have used it in what goes before, is not, of course, properly opposed to the word " journalist." The best journalist, other things being equal, is he who uses most " artistry " in doing what he has to do. But in real life the distinction does well enough: the journalist writes on day-to-day subjects, and, as a rule, has not time to be much of an artist. However, to prove that Mr. Wells has considerable artistic powers is not·to prove that he is anything more than an unusually good journalist. I should like to show, if I can, that he has been very much more at his best; but the right descriptive word is not easy to find. The German language allows one to use of a prose-writer the word *Dichter*, " poet," which we are obliged to translate clumsily and inadequately " creative artist." If I were to say that many of Mr. Wells's early books have a poetic quality I should run the risk of conveying a false impression. Luckily they have a peculiar quality which enables them to bear a special description. They are, in their degree, myths; and Mr. Wells is a myth-maker.

Mr. Beresford says, in his essay on Mr. Wells, that *The Island of Dr. Moreau* does not intend

158

"any particular fable beyond the evident one that, physically, one species is as like to the next as makes no matter." But the story, I think, reaches further than that. There is a remote island, where no ship ever touches, ruled by an old, outlawed scientist pursuing without ruth his inquiries into the plasticity of living flesh. Its population is brutes, brought a second time into the world in " the House of Pain " in horrible human semblance, suffering ignorantly from the conflict between their bestial instincts and the law which has been imposed on them. If they break it, they return to the operating-table. Moreau is killed. The brute instincts, relieved from fear of him, begin to rise again and the Beast Folk gradually slide back to their origins. The only human survivor finds his way back to England, stricken in mind, with a shrinking from human beings. He says, in the course of his adventures on the island:—

" A strange persuasion came over me that, save for the grossness of the line, the grotesqueness of the forms, I had here before me the whole balance of human life in miniature, the whole interplay of instinct, reason and fate in its simplest form. "

And when he reaches England again, the thought recurs:—

" I look about me at my fellow-men. And I go in fear. I see faces keen and bright, others dull or dangerous, others unsteady, insincere; none that have the calm authority of a reasonable soul. I feel as though the animal was surging up through them; that presently the degradation of the Islanders will be played over again on a larger

scale. I know this is an illusion, that these seeming
men and women about me are indeed men and
women, men and women for ever, perfectly reasonable creatures, full of human desires and tender
solicitude, emancipated from instinct, and the
slaves of no fantastic Law—beings altogether
different from the Beast Folk. Yet I shrink from
them, from their curious glances, their inquiries
and assistance, and long to be away from them and
alone."

These passages suggest one interpretation of the
book. But it is a myth, not an allegory; and,
whereas an allegory bears a single and definite
interpretation, a myth does not, but can be interpreted in many ways, none of them quite consistent,
all of them more alive and fruitful than the rigid
allegorical correspondence. This work is a conspicuous example of Mr. Wells's work in his
character of myth-maker; and it is among the
half-dozen or so things, two of them at least being
short stories, which, I believe, constitute his permanent contribution to English literature.

Among the short stories, *The Country of the Blind*
ranks as high. There is a lost valley in the Andes
where a body of settlers was cut off by an earth-
quake. Some influence in the air of the place
affected their eyes. They multiplied, and the new
generation was born blind, and succeeding generations forgot what " seeing " meant. Into this
valley falls by accident a Peruvian guide. There
are legends of it in his country, and he thinks
he will make himself king in this kingdom of the
blind. But he is not prepared against the special
acuteness of sense which the blind people have
developed; and he finds himself not their king,
but their inferior and their butt. At last he resigns

himself and desires to marry one of their daughters. The wise men agree that his foolishness is probably caused by two useless protuberances under his forehead and decide that, if these are removed, the match may be permitted. He accepts the condition—but when its fulfilment is due he revolts and flies. Again a myth, with all its subtly shifting possibilities of interpretation.

I do not know whether any one has ever noticed the odd resemblance between this tale and one by Remy de Gourmont. The comparison is exceedingly interesting. Gourmont is a teller of fairy-tales in the old manner: he imagines "a distant country" where strange conditions obtain. But Mr. Wells is the myth-maker of the scientific modern world. As the Greeks found material for their mythology in the nature which surrounded them, so he finds his in the scientific atmosphere of the twentieth century. No fairy-tale country for him, nor anything inconsistent with biological possibilities! The settlers "did not think of germs and infection"; but Mr. Wells does. And the consequences of the "strange disease" that blinded them are worked out in complete accordance with what we know of the adaptability of human intelligence. The other and very important point of contrast with Mr. Wells's story, with its significance undefined and well clothed in concrete detail, is larger and more suggestive than Gourmont's more satirical, less living version.

I think Mr. Wells's last successful attempt to create a myth on a large scale was *The Food of the Gods*. The struggle between the new huge growth, rats like mastiffs, wasps as big as hens and men forty feet high, and the old little world is simply a modern version, from a different angle and in scientific terms, of what an earlier writer attempted in terms of the Greek mythology:—

" As Heaven and Earth are fairer, fairer far
   Than Chaos and blank Darkness, though once
      chiefs;
   And as we show beyond that Heaven and Earth
In form and shape compact and beautiful,
In will, in action free, companionship,
And thousand other signs of purer life;
So on our heels a fresh perfection treads."

Mr. Wells's politicians and scare-raising journalists and men talking in railway carriages seem very different from Keats's fallen Titans; but the idea which they embody is the same.

IV

It is dangerous work guessing what turned Mr. Wells's mind from work of this order to work in his later manner. The change is from the eternal to the temporal. Before and after it he wrote novels which were not scientific romances and yet not " problem novels." These are books about the romance of ordinary existence and there are five of them in all—*The Wheels of Chance*, which is an unripe precursor of two more, *Kipps* and *Mr. Polly*, *Love and Mr. Lewisham*, a story with traces of Gissing about it which its author, I think, over-rates, and that lamentably facetious work, *Bealby*. Of these *Mr. Polly* in its gusto, its rich, wandering, picaresque invention, is undoubtedly the best: it is like *Æpyornis Island*, another entertainment devised by a modern Scheherazade.

But most of his novels since about 1906 have been clearly didactic, propagandist and controversial in nature. They are written " about " contemporary topics: the characters are invented to discuss and illustrate contemporary problems. Mr. Wells has shifted his focus from the human spirit to the difficulties which the human spirit finds itself in at the moment. *Marriage* is " about " marriage: *Ann Veronica* is " about " the relations between parents and children and also " about " love and sex: *Joan and Peter* is " about " the bringing-up of children and adolescents: *The Soul of a Bishop* is " about " modern developments in religion. Now, debatable question as it is and not to be argued in an essay of this scope, I believe that Mr. Wells's business as an artist is not with these surface things, but with the fundamentals in human nature which produce them and on which they react. No doubt a writer with something urgent to say is at liberty to choose his way of saying it—provided that he succeeds. But does Mr. Wells (if we use the word in a full and far-seeing sense) really succeed ? I think that the books of which I am speaking are made up of a jumble of general opinions on conduct and of special cases. The general opinions would have been clearer if they had been stated as such by themselves: the confirmation which they seem to get by being associated with the special cases is only specious: and the special cases are only intermittently pictures of living human beings, since they are always at the mercy of the arguments they illustrate. Mr. Wells never plays quite fair with his characters here: no artist who turns to propaganda ever can do so. True, these books are readable; but Mr. Wells is too good a writer not to be readable, whatever handicap he may assume.

163

Besides, much of the lack of grip of his later novels, to which I shall refer again, seems to be due to his mistaken use of his powers. If it be argued that his later books do interest more readers than his earlier books, I assert that it will not be so in the long run.

Tono-Bungay, which to a certain extent begins this series, is Mr. Wells's last novel of high rank, and it is only a little " about " patent medicines and advertising and company promoting. It is a panoramic view of our modern civilisation. George Ponderevo began life in the housekeeper's room at Bladesover and rose to be " an item in the house-party of a countess "; he speaks of " this remarkable social range, this extensive cross-section of the British social organism." That is the value of his story; and his story does make one definite, though complex impression, in spite of his desire " to get into it all sorts of things that struck me, things that amused me and impressions that I got—even although they don't minister directly to my narrative at all." This sounds like Mr. Wells's antici-patory defence of his new loose method of writing; but here it is hardly necessary. *Tono-Bungay* is a description, in a multitude of instances, of how human nature expressed itself in England in the twentieth century; and, because the emphasis is still on the fundamental nature behind the expres-sion, it has the unity without which a book cannot be fully interesting. But already the emphasis is beginning to shift.

Ponderevo's excuse for *Tono-Bungay* being written " all over the place," as one says, was that it was his first novel and almost certainly his last. But that defence is no good for Mr. Wells and, there-fore, he has written an essay on some length on

The Work of Mr. H. G. Wells

The Contemporary Novel. Here he attacks " that tired giant, the prosperous Englishman," who " wants to be taken out of himself " and " doesn't want—*Problems.*" Well, that gentleman is sufficiently catered for by other writers than Mr. Wells, and we need not take much account of him. But the essay goes on to attack the critics who allege that this or that book " isn't a novel," and to urge " a return to the lax freedom of form, the rambling discursiveness, the right to roam " of an earlier age. " Nothing is irrelevant," it argues, " if the writer's mood is happy." And Mr. Wells curiously puts forward *The Old Wives' Tale*, that strict, tight, perfectly proportioned book, as an example of roaming, rambling fiction.

Now no one has a right to demand form in the novel except in so far as he finds the author's attention to form a means of pinning his interest; and no one has a right to condemn irrelevancies in a novel unless he finds them making it duller than it should have been. Mr. Wells mistakes the " laws " of criticism, which are, in fact, generalisations from multitudes of observations, for rules arbitrarily imposed. Critical " laws " are precisely like scientific " laws ": they are valid only so long as no new fact upsets them. Mr. Wells's recent novels do not upset, I think, the generalisations that a work of art to be interesting must have a unity, a centre, must pursue a definite object, as patiently and single-mindedly as Mr. Bennett pursues his object in *The Old Wives' Tale*.

The subject of that book is the growing up and the growing old of two sisters, it is the progress, shown in these two examples, of humanity from youth to age. What is the subject of Mr. Wells's *Joan and Peter* ? One begins to answer confusedly:

Education and the various methods of bringing up the young in England, with discursions on Imperialism, on the war, on sex problems, and on other things. Education is the nearest approach to a centre that the book contains; but it does not approach very near. The development of Joan and Peter is *not* the subject. When, for example, Peter finds Joan at Cambridge consorting with an Indian student and is troubled, the emphasis is thrown, not on the significance this has for both their spirits, but on the general question of white and coloured races. If a critic looks at this book as impartially as he can and finds that it does not interest him as much as it should, considering the brilliance with which it is written, what is he to conclude? He may well defend the conclusion that still the " law " holds good that a novel to be interesting must pursue a definite object. He will add perhaps that Mr. Wells's original object seems to have been the present state of education in England, but that it did not lend itself to treatment in fiction.

I am not so sure as I am of this of the further conclusion that a wrong choice of subjects accounts for many defects in the style of these novels—for the amazing verbosity of *Joan and Peter*, out of which thousands of words could be " sweated " without eliminating one incident or one argument, for such grotesque devices as the calling in of an angel into the North Library of the Athenæum Club in order to convert the Bishop of Princhester to the ideas of *God the Invisible King*, for the tendency to forget a minor character and introduce him again with a new set of qualities. But I strongly suspect it. A radical evil will produce many on the surface; and the radical evil of these

166

books is that they are " not novels " but a sort of literary mules, doomed to sterility and bad tempers. It is even possible to find in Mr. Wells's last " novel " signs of his recognition that the bastard form will not do: for *The Undying Fire* is no more a novel than *The Republic* or Dryden's *Essay of Dramatic Poesy*. It is quite simply a philosophical dialogue.

It is true that " uninteresting " seems a rather unsuitable epithet of condemnation to apply to these books; but I think it is fundamentally just. The immediate urgency of their topics makes them deceptively readable; but when that urgency has passed they will be readable no longer, except for those brilliant individual passages which each one of them contains. Even already, *Ann Veronica*, published in 1908, is beginning to fade, true and admirable as are many of its passages. It treated notions current in that year about sex-problems and the relations between parents and children as though they were of universal validity. This book was of the surface only; and the surface has changed.

v

This is not the place, if I had the room and the competence, for an exhaustive criticism of Mr. Wells's political, moral, and religious ideas; but a general sketch of the character of his thought is necessary. Its predominating colour is that of impatience. He once delivered a lecture which he called *The Discovery of the Future*. One of the most remarkable things about him, as I have already noted, is that the past has no native roots in his mind; and it might be said that the future has taken its place. It is natural for a man so constituted to be impatient. He can foresee in an hour more than can happen in a century; and he demands that the procession shall be accelerated. He is perpetually in the position of a child on Christmas Eve: he finds that the hours go very slowly to Christmas morning. He has, indeed, through the mouth of one of his characters, Karenin in *The World Set Free*, preached patience with human slowness; but after all there are few points of view which he has not preached at one time or another. Karenin's effect on his listeners was doubtful: on his creator it has been quite negligible.

It would be interesting if an investigator would some day trace the rise of that nineteenth century rage for prophesying which culminated in the liberal vaticinations of Mr. Wells. The " discovery of the future " was a good phrase. The nineteenth century discovered it almost as definitely as Columbus discovered America: until then it was thought of roughly as an unchanged continuation of the present. And, before Mr. Wells's *Anticipations*, prophecy was hardly organised or methodical: it was mostly a method of finding a locality for your Utopia. But Mr. Wells has prophesied more ardently, more often and more fully than any one before or since. His first book of forecasts, written about 1900, is still readable and in many ways has proved astonishingly correct. He foresaw the splashing out, instead of the spreading, of the great towns over the surrounding country-side. He foresaw the development of road-transport. So far as flying was concerned, he imagined slower than events have gone, but how much faster than any one else imagined! He pictured a different type of machine from any that has appeared; but his visualisation of aerial warfare turned out to be strangely correct.

Then after twenty years of looking forward over the history of the world from the moment in which he happened to be writing, he turned back and surveyed it from its beginnings. This wonderful book—which phrase I use without forgetting its defects—is certainly the work of a man whose chief interest lies in the future. Mr. Wells sets about all the past ages with just so much zest as he might find in tidying a cluttered writing-table. It would have been considerably better if in several places he had adopted a different point of view. But, in spite of its defects, it was very much better that *The Outline of History* should have been written than that it should not; and who else could have done it with so much chance of success and influence? This is among his perishable works, for others, it can hardly be doubted, will follow him and rewrite his history without his peculiar biases. But he has established the framework, as it has never yet been done, since, under the influence of Ranke, history took on the methods of science, multiplied its material a hundredfold and passed out of the hands of men of letters and imagination.

The radical fault of the *Outline* is, of course, merely its impatience. One seems to hear Mr. Wells saying: You talk of your Greece and Rome! Poor fools, who had not even enough wit to invent the Penny Post! Mankind has been on the earth some twenty thousand years and even now (for to such details does his Utopia condescend) the practice is not universal of rounding the corners of rooms and the edges of floors and ceilings for convenience in dusting. It is an unfortunate fact that Mr. Wells often seems to find himself in the position of scold to the entire human race.

In an impatient man, a man always in a hurry, we are not surprised to find the allied defect of instability. Some one once said that it was Mr. Wells's habit " to conduct his own education in public ": he himself, I believe, invented the expression " provisional thinking." One sometimes wishes that he could educate himself a little more privately, that he would keep his provisional thoughts a little longer in his notebook. But he is a man of ideas; and when he has an idea to express he proceeds to express it with all his persuasive powers. A disciple would be hard put to it to ascertain his final views on the sex-problems he has so often solved. The just men made perfect by an unknown gas in a comet's tail admit a sort of group-marriage as a conceivable solution of some of them. The hero of *The New Machiavelli* seems to arrive at a comparative chastity by a process of trial and error. George Ponderevo's love-affair with Beatrice is a justificatory study in æsthetic sensuality. Peter's trials and errors with Hettie are severely reprobated. And, one may be allowed to observe, if the propagation of right ideas can do any good then the propagation of wrong ideas must do harm. All the ideas Mr. Wells has put forward on political and social topics cannot be right.

His defence might be that the good done by right ideas is greater than all the harm wrong ideas can ever do. It is perhaps at any rate a tolerable defence that he is a man of many ideas. His impatience, his restlessness, and his haste carry him incessantly round the modern world and nothing that is topical is alien to him: there is no subject which may not inspire him to demand of the thinking public that it should stop and think about it. Even where he causes repulsion, as his glib and facile assertions often do, that is of itself a stimulus to thought.

In this brief essay I have omitted much I should have liked to include. I have said next to nothing, for example, of his humour, of the rollicking adventures of Kipps and Mr. Polly, or of the malicious but admirably satirical portrait gallery which is contained in *The New Machiavelli*. I have said nothing of his gift of descriptive phrase, which can illuminate the dreariest argument. But it would be pusillanimous to close a study of so eminent a prophet without some prophecy of his future reputation. This will, I imagine, resemble very closely one of those eighteenth-century reputations which have not many books to show in justification of themselves. Mr. Wells will seem to have been a great figure in the intellectual life of his time; but his books will be ruthlessly winnowed. I should select for possible survival *The Island of Dr. Moreau* and *The Food of the Gods*, *The Invisible Man* and, perhaps, *The Time Machine*, *Tono-Bungay*, and *Mr. Polly*, and possibly all the short stories collected with *The Country of the Blind*, but certainly that one and *The Green Door*. I think future readers will pay as much and as little attention to *Ann Veronica* and the rest of them as we do to the tragedies of Voltaire: students will read them in order to be able to declare that no one else need do so. For the rest—a vigorous and restless thinker who powerfully disturbed the waters of his generation.

Reflections on the Recent History of the English Novel

MR. LASCELLES ABERCROMBIE has remarked, in his study of Mr. Hardy, that the novel is the most recent growth in literature. Mr. Max Beerbohm drives this home by his translation of Dr. Johnson's comparison of eighteenth-century sermon-writers into a comparison of modern novelists. " ' Yes, sir,' some great pundit may be telling a disciple at this moment, ' Wells is one of the best, Galsworthy is one of the best, if you except his concern for delicacy of style. Mrs. Ward has a very firm grasp of problems, but is not very creational.— Caine's books are very edifying. I should like to read all that Caine has written. Miss Corelli, too, is very edifying.—And you may add Upton Sinclair.' " We do not, so runs Mr. Beerbohm's moral, read sermons much to-day. Will our descendants in the next century look back on our novels and our painstaking discriminations between this novelist and that as something incomprehensible and slightly amusing ? For this latest growth of time has not had the long history it might have had, and it may disappear as it came. Between the *Satyricon* and *Clarissa* the form was invented and reinvented often enough; but no generation, until the second half of the eighteenth century, was so deeply impressed by its possibilities as to explore them. Then all the world began to write novels, including the greatest men of the time—Goethe, Rousseau, Scott. Within a hundred years it was the chief medium of literary expression in all Western countries. Now we are receiving novels from every people on the earth—Hindu novels and Japanese novels and Negro novels.

It must always be remembered that the cascade of prose fiction which flows spring and autumn from the presses is not invariably due to the unaided working of the time-spirit in the minds of authors. The modern public is willing to devour novels: it is not willing to devour much else: it is supplied with novels. The individual drops in the flood are not often created by a quite spontaneous impulse in the writer, even when he is a serious and conscientious artist. It is said that nowadays the author who has written even a very promising first novel will find some difficulty in getting it published. It is certain that the author of any other kind of first book is in a far worse position. Therefore the man with ideas to express, equally with the man who has a career to make, is led to the novel —because the novel is undoubtedly more in demand than any other form of literature.

Moreover, sordid as the thought may seem, it means money. The writer of verses, if he has a reputation and can find a publisher and has a little luck besides, may earn enough by the publication of his biennial volume to keep him in cigarettes for one out of the two years. The number of men under fifty who have earned enough by a collection of poems to buy a cottage could be counted on the fingers of one hand. Some writers (not many) do actually live on the proceeds of their novels. Others, who, if left to themselves, would never attempt the form of prose fiction, are driven to do so in the hope, if not of making their fortunes, then at least of augmenting their incomes. It is, apart from periodical journalism, the most serious and probable

173

way of entering literature as a profession; and, whether we like it or not, literature is a profession and most of our good writers are, as they always have been, professional writers. Let us add to these considerations the fact that there are many clever men who can, and successfully do, practise the writing of stories purely as a trade. All these points are, no doubt, sordid enough, but they are not irrelevant. They exercise a far-reaching influence on literature in general and the novel in particular; and they immensely complicate the material with which a critic has to deal when he wishes to discover what the novel is at present and whither it is going.

Their influence on literature is not hard to discern. It would be odious, if it were possible, to take examples from among living authors; but let us recall John Davidson. Davidson was a poet whose merits were recognised, in his own day as in ours, more by lip-service than by any solid tribute. I believe that first editions of some of his books can still be obtained from their publishers, while many others have not been thought worth reprinting. It must have been in despair of gaining any reward from his poetry, not from any natural inclination, that he turned to writing novels; and he wrote a string of them.[1] None of these books has any

[1] Mr. Scott Moncrieff disagrees and points out that Davidson began the writing of novels early in his career and early abandoned it, and also that his reputation was made by his poems. I do not see that this in the least invalidates my argument, which is founded, I admit, on a pure guess at Davidson's motives. It need not have taken him long to surmise how little poetry would give : it need not have taken him long to find out that, for him, novel-writing would be an inefficient crutch. I made my guess to account for his novels which, I still maintain, have all the appearance of being written by a man totally unfitted for that form of literature and pursuing it reluctantly. I may be wrong about Davidson; but no one will deny that there are many such cases.

174

real value. The best of them, *Baptist Lake*, is a jumbled farrago, betraying by its fatigued incoherence a talent forced into use in one department of literature, though nature and the proclivities of its owner would have had it employed in another. And Davidson's case, though it is extreme, can be paralleled by many others in a greater or lesser degree. Yet the circumstances which make it obligatory on, say, seven writers out of every ten to try their hands at the novel are not altogether without beneficial results. Prose fiction is at least certain of drawing within its compass almost all the available talent of any given generation, whether suitable or not. It is refreshed and kept lively by the intrusion of alien points of view, by a constant a vigorous process of cross-breeding. John Davidson's stories were not satisfactory as prose fiction or as works of their author; but they contained elements of poetry and fantasy in which the English novel has not always been rich and which it is now beginning to exhibit again more prominently.

The effect on the critic is, of course, simply to confuse him. Figures are available (though not at this moment to me) showing how many novels are published every year in England: there cannot be fewer than five hundred. Twenty years, to go no farther back—ten thousand novels. You may see them on the shelves of circulating libraries in seaside towns; but the weaker vessels, to the number of nine thousand or thereabouts, you will not see anywhere else. Yet among these relegated volumes are some which we praised when they first appeared, which we read with refreshment, in which we found ingenuity, beauty, liveliness. One can never forget that each of them took, on an average, a year to compose and was read, on an average, in five or six hours—and probably never again by the same person. One is reminded of the Chinaman's description of tobogganing—" Shoo! Whizz! Bang!—walkee back two mile." The reader forgets the book he has just finished, and the author begins another.

These faded covers at the back of the stationer's shop are distressing to regard, but here is the texture in which a few golden threads must be distinguished. Here are masterpieces, would-be masterpieces, novels written for the public which take its fancy, novels written for the public which do not even do that. There is nowhere any clear line of demarcation. Few books appear in which no genuine breath of impulse can be felt. Many appear in which genuine impulse and the adventitious attractions of the novel seem to be mixed in equal parts. Surprisingly many thrust their heads a little out of the enormous ruck. The critic, contemplating this medley, is tempted to exclaim that there is no tendency, no main stream, that the innovations are not new and the examples have no effect.

And yet, a year or two before the war, voices were raised to announce that we had a new and rising school of novelists. The genius of Henry James was beginning to set, mists of thickening obscurity floating across the splendid disc, which, because of them and because it was so near to the horizon, looked more impressive than ever before. But Henry James in the novel seems just now to have been what Voltaire once called a certain historical occurrence—" a great event without consequences." Mr. Hardy had not published a novel for some fifteen years—a fact which even then few persons seemed to have realised. Mr. Conrad was wondering, not without reason, whether he had not become the novelist of a restricted clique of admirers. The two great reputations then establishing themselves were those of Mr. Wells and Mr. Bennett. Behind these authors came a number of younger men, among whom may be named Mr. J. D. Beresford, Mr. Compton Mackenzie, Mr. Hugh Walpole, Mr. D. H. Lawrence, Mr. Frank Swinnerton—there were several others.

Mr. Wells and Mr. Bennett ruled between them the world of the progressive novel and were admired, perhaps equally, by their juniors; but their methods were fundamentally different. Both were reprobated as realists, yet each wrote and composed his stories with an intention reaching beyond the mere presentation of life as he saw it. Mr. Wells, from *Tono-Bungay* onwards, devoted himself to the exposition of practical ideas, to getting things done. He trampled on the definitions of the novels that were occasionally offered to him. He hoped by means of the weapon of prose fiction to assail the capitalist system, to overhaul religion, and to alter the relations of the sexes. The art of the novel became in his hands an applied art. But Mr. Bennett strove in almost all his books to express a single truth which bore not on present society but on the life of the individual now and at all times. He strove to express his belief in the wonder and romance of ordinary existence, the idea that to any man the action of getting married is so exciting that Napoleon's first victory can be, even to Napoleon, hardly more so. Two books of his at least, the *Old Wives' Tale* and *Clayhanger*, presented this conception almost perfectly. He had studied the French realists; and at times he appeared to accept the " slice-of-life " label which, whether for praise or blame, was regularly affixed to him. But realism, even with the French and German exponents of that school, was never actually much more than a question of technique; and with Mr. Bennett it was never anything more. The two books I have named, and indeed all that he has written (with the exception, perhaps, of *The Pretty Lady*), are thoroughly romantic in temper. They are examples of deliberate cunning selection and composition; and in each the story is so presented that it has what can be called only a definitely poetic significance. These books, that is to say, express single emotions: they do not merely portray life as it is, they also create a new kind of life.

Mr. Wells had been a romantic, a poet, in his time. There was no realism in *The Time Machine*, *The Island of Dr. Moreau*, or *The Invisible Man*. These were poetic visions, though, once the fantastic premises were established, the details were worked out with realistic exactitude. But early in the new century Mr. Wells indicated unmistakably his desire to write for time instead of eternity, to satirise the weaknesses and relieve the distresses of the existing moment. Not long before 1914, in a novel of didactic intentions, *The War in the Air*, he achieved, for the last time, a purely poetic effect in a vision of what the world might come to if its peoples could not find a way of keeping the peace. This was as good a thing of its kind as Mr. Wells (and the words " or anybody else " are almost superfluous) has ever done. Since then Mr. Wells the artist has almost disappeared: we have had in his place only the preacher and the publicist. This is not an accusation. Any man is at liberty to do what he pleases with his own gifts; and if one

178

attacks Mr. Wells for his use of them it must be on the ground he himself has chosen, which lies outside the range of these observations. It remains to be noted that, with a degeneration in style which makes one think of a middle-aged man " losing his figure," he has retained the realistic method in telling so much of a story as he still cares to tell. He still, between the passages of argument, carries on the narrative, and makes it convincing, by means of detail exactly observed and accurately stated. But his books are ceasing to have the form of novels —a novel can be defined only as an extended prose narrative describing the actions of imaginary persons —and are becoming modern versions of the philosophical dialogue. *The Undying Fire* was nothing else; and whatever present or future this form may have it does not concern me here.

I do not know whether I have properly made clear the attempted distinction between realism as a means and realism as an end in itself. The word is one of those convenient but treacherous instruments of criticism which cannot be both defined and exemplified. Produce a logical and self-consistent definition, and you will find that you have defined all possible examples into some other camp. Name your examples, and you will find that no definition can embrace them all. More even than Mr. Wells and Mr. Bennett, Mr. Galsworthy has been praised or blamed as a realist of photographic fidelity. Yet he certainly has intentions beyond the representation of life as it is, because he has always desired to castigate by satire or direct reproof our contemporary manners and morals. Such a title as *The Island Pharisees* tells its own story. And where he has been most photographic, with all the advantages the theatre can give him, as in the police-court scene in *The Silver Box*, where every detail of setting and procedure is as accurate as observation can make it, he deliberately tilts the balance of probability to emphasise the sufferings of the poor and the callousness of the rich. It has been commonly urged against the realists that they arrange their material as much as the most arrant romantic, that they arrange it to present only a dreary and squalid appearance. Mr. Beerbohm has drawn Mr. Galsworthy " looking on life and seeing that it is foul." This means that Mr. Galsworthy looks at life from a very personal and not at all impartial standpoint. But it must be owned that he was never only a realist even in this debased and reproachful sense of the word. His portraits of old men and young girls are enough to protect him against the charge: for he has sometimes treated these subjects with dignified and beautiful sentiment. His more recent books (until the latest, *To Let*) unfortunately have been of a sort that does not illustrate any tendency in the artistically serious novel.

Where, then, is the true realist, the impassive recorder of life as it is ? Certainly a new style of novel has appeared which comes closer to this than anything Mr. Galsworthy or Mr. Bennett or Mr. Wells has ever written. Mr. James Joyce, Mrs. Virginia Woolf, Miss Dorothy Richardson, and, in France, M. Marcel Proust have composed works which are examples of almost pure, unbiased portrayal. They do not, indeed, show us life as it is, a thing as unattainable as absolute truth; but they do come near to showing us life as it presents itself to a single consciousness. Their books have no other aim, no plot to develop, no idea to expound. M. Proust's *A la Recherche du Temps Perdu*, where

180

it is not padded with portentously trivial psychology, gives us an image of life, seen, as it were, on the screen of a camera obscura, diminutive, vivid, and amusing. His style may have had—I do not know —some influence on Mr. Joyce and Mrs. Wolff, who in certain respects resemble him. It is unlikely that he has had any on Miss Richardson, and a comparison of her work with that of the writers I have grouped with her is instructive.

The experiences—one can hardly call them adventures—of Miriam Henderson are now in their fifth or sixth volume.[1] It would seem that Miss Richardson cannot write them as fast as they happen. Their merit is in their absolute, immediately convincing fidelity to fact. Their demerit is in their lack of interest. There are incidents in the story, such incidents as happen to Miriam, and there is humour, such humour as Miriam finds in her daily life. But the incidents that happen to Miriam are not exciting and her capacity for finding humour in life is not great. The value of an exact record of life as it appears to a single consciousness must depend on the value of that consciousness. Apparently the ability to render an accurate and convincing account of sensations does not involve the possession of any other quality. An exact record of life as it appears to a bore will be boring; an exact record of life as it appears to a wit will be witty. M. Proust, Mrs. Woolf, and Mr. Joyce have written witty books. These writers represent in a sense a new sort of realism; but it is not certain that their discovery will have much effect on the progress of the novel. Already in *Ulysses*,

[1] As this book will be two or three months printing, I cannot guarantee that these statistics will remain accurate when it appears.

or such chapters of it as I have had an opportunity of reading,[1] Mr. Joyce appears to me to be passing over into a new kind of art. Here cerebral force and sensitiveness of perception are raised as much above what we find in real life as the emotions of the romantics above those of common experience. The heroes of Rousseau had hypertrophied hearts: perhaps Mr. Joyce's future heroes will be found to have hypertrophied heads. They must certainly (though this is by the way) have hypertrophied olfactory nerves.

Realism in this sense, then, does exist, though it is rare and perhaps not stable. The younger novelists of 1913 and thereabouts were realists in another and looser sense. As applied to them the word means only that they drew their material from ordinary life, from a range of experience familiar to themselves and their readers. In this they were followers of Mr. Wells and Mr. Bennett, but they had not much else in common with the elder writers or with one another. This at least they had. When Mr. Walpole wrote his Russian books it was not with the object of finding a scene out of common knowledge where his imagination could have free play. It was rather his purpose to bring that scene inside common knowledge—to give a picture of Russian life and character which would make them comprehensible to English readers. The persons in his English books are mostly normal English types. Mr. Compton Mackenzie, in a more flowery way, writes also of normal English types. He seeks, with an amount of vitality which most of his contemporaries might envy and which seems too often to be misapplied, rather to impose a romantic

[1] *Ulysses* has now appeared as a whole. But one cannot deal with *Ulysses* in a foot-note.

colour on his material than to draw it thence—a method which stands in strong contrast with that of Mr. Bennett. The manner of *Clayhanger* appears, with some differences, in Mr. Frank Swinnerton's beautiful *Nocturne*.

One more characteristic can be attributed, without more than incidental injustice, to what was a group only in virtue of the accidental contemporaneity of its members. Their main interest is in the portrayal and development of character rather than in the telling of a story or in the creation of an atmosphere or even in the events produced by a clash of characters. Their narrative invention appears more piecemeal than in the whole and is of subordinate importance. The reader's attention is focused less on what happens than on how the characters behave. It is, that is to say, the novel of psychology. The events of Mr. Beresford's *God's Counterpoint* might be altered from beginning to end and yet the centre of gravity of the book would remain unchanged. It is the life of Philip Manning, who, from circumstances of his childhood, received a mental twist which coloured his whole career and poisoned his married life until it was straightened. There are various scenes and episodes—the death of his father, a publisher's office, the purchase of a house. These exist, have been devised, simply to illustrate Philip's character and its evolution. No doubt Mr. Beresford has chosen the scenes and episodes best fitted to his purpose: the book could not otherwise have been the deep, disturbing, and engrossing study of personality which in fact it is. But another set of illustrations is conceivable and would not have changed its nature or its theme, though it might have injured its quality.

First Essays on Literature

This is a characteristic work of the period under review, one of the best it has produced. There are many exceptions to be made to the judgment which it exemplifies. Mr. Beresford himself, an experimental and changing author, has written novels of quite a different kind—*The Hampdenshire Wonder*, a philosophical fantasy, *The Jervaise Comedy*, a complete and rounded episode, reminiscent in its general lines of Henry James. Mr. D. H. Lawrence, though the presentment of psychology has been his chief interest, has a remarkable power of creating an emotional atmosphere and of intensifying it by its setting. The end of *The Lost Girl*, a description of an Englishwoman's life with an Italian peasant, is an excellent specimen of his achievement in this direction. In his last book, *Women in Love*, he appears to be making in the direction of types and abstractions and mythological figures—which, however, he still seeks (unfortunately, as I think) to clothe in the circumstances of everyday. But the judgment is, I believe, essentially correct. These writers have concerned themselves chiefly so far with character, whether, as in *God's Counterpoint*, that of a single person, or, as in Mr. Walpole's *Secret City*, that of a Russian household, or, as in Mr. Swinnerton's *Shops and Houses*, that of a London suburb. Some power of situation and atmosphere there must be; but this is of subordinate importance. And these writers use the realistic *method*. They choose their incidents, compose their pictures; but they substantiate their incidents by accurately detailed descriptions of things as we know them in everyday life.

This, it may be objected, leaves every novelist a practitioner of realism: the word means no more

184

than that the incidents and characters are made to
seem probable. And it may be argued that the
nature of the novel, the key in which it is written
and read, renders this inevitable. The objection
brings me to the name of the author whom I
should choose as the most significant figure in the
English novel of to-day. Mr. Conrad is not a
realist. Indeed his books are of so distinctive a
kind that one is tempted to speak wildly about
them, to remove them from the category of novels,
and affirm that they are epics written in prose.
But it is wise to cling to definitions. The novel is
an extended prose narrative describing the actions
of imaginary persons; and Mr. Conrad's books
are novels, precisely as Mr. Wells's later books are
not. But his persons are not conceived on the
same plane as those of novelists who use the realistic
method; and " epic " is not a bad word to describe
their nature. Lingard in *The Rescue*, Winnie,
Verloc, and the idiot in *The Secret Agent* are not
realistically conceived or painted. They are simpli-
fied in the epic manner and are made to transcend
humanity while remaining true to it.

As it is one of the functions of great art not
merely to portray life but also to create a new,
inexisting but possible life, it is in general necessary
for the great artist to suggest in his scenes and
characters some remoteness from the life we all
know. The Greeks found this remoteness in the
legends of their heroic age, and many writers have
continued more or less fruitfully to use the same
convention. The Elizabethan dramatists made use
of Italy and so established a narrower, less general
convention which has been disastrous to most of
their successors. The danger of this procedure in
the hands of little men is obvious, but it is no less

185

desirable for great men. The characters of great art must be human if they are to interest us vitally; but human beings as we know them are restricted and stunted by many influences. If, therefore, these characters are to take on qualities ideally great, whether in good or in evil, they must be removed into a sphere where we are not perpetually reminded of the everyday world. They must be allowed to develop their greatness, unhampered by time or circumstance. In many of his books, Mr. Conrad fulfils this condition by choosing settings which are unfamiliar at least to his readers, by isolating his characters to work out their fates in strange places. Lingard and his companions in the lagoon where the tragedy of *The Rescue* is enacted, Lord Jim on his island, even Captain Macwhirr, picked up, as it were, between finger and thumb of the typhoon—these persons grow in isolation to more than human stature. *The Secret Agent* shows this method and its opposite in sharp relief, because it is written on both planes. On the one side we have the world of drawing-rooms, Home Secretaries, and Commissioners of Police—a not unfamiliar world; and here the book is little better than a *roman policer* composed by a superbly adroit writer. On the other side is the strange secluded underworld of anarchy and espionage, where wickedness and maternal love and even stupidity can assume ideal proportions; and this part of the book is written by a great artist.

With Mr. Conrad the portrayal of a character is not so pre-eminent a consideration as with the writers I have just been describing. I do not mean that his characters are insufficiently or conventionally drawn : they are indeed extremely vivid and original. But the book is not about them solely,

186

but about the events which their natures produce. One might almost say that, instead of the situation being invented to display them, they are invented to support the situation. The centre of gravity of Mr. Conrad's novels lies in action and situation; and here he coincides with a tendency which was already in operation before he began to influence it. The narrative gift, the faculty of telling a story, is taking with renewed importance its place in the development of the novel.

And the human appetite for plot, for incident ingeniously contrived, developed, and resolved, is not a negligible thing. The inability of a novelist to invent or manage a plot is rather like the inability of a musician to invent a tune. It may be compatible with many great qualities, even with greatness in the absolute sense, but it is a sign of a certain elementary deficiency. Mr. D. H. Lawrence is entitled (in the improbable event of his caring to do so) to look down on Miss Ethel Dell as his inferior. He can write English, she does not. His intentions are artistically serious, hers are not. But Miss Dell can tell a story, and he in general does not. It is true that Miss Dell is spoilt for you and me and (very likely) Mr. Lawrence by fatuities and insincerities and vulgarities which it would be wearisome to enumerate. But a great public reads Miss Dell, not because she is fatuous and insincere and vulgar, but because she can and does tell a story.

It is the danger of the artist that the exceptional qualities which make him what he is naturally seduce him into becoming a little inhuman, into an estrangement from common and fundamental desires. Only on the stage is he brought rigorously to test. There, whatever the protestations of himself and his admirers, he must satisfy to some extent the normal appetite or he must cease to exist. And the drama and the novel have so close a resemblance that hardly in more than technical details does what is true of the one cease to be true of the other. Consider, then, the culmination of Shakespeare's career. What is it but one attempt after another to express himself by means of a plot, of a story, ending with the complete success of *The Tempest*? For many years, however, so far as story-telling goes, the hungry sheep have looked up and have been at the best inadequately fed. Stevenson wrote romances of adventure which were also works of literature. Since his time good writers have been strangely little moved to experiment in the same direction. But the story of adventure, as exemplified by *The Master of Ballantrae* or even by some of Mr. Conrad's books, is not the whole of the matter. The genius of narrative is simply the ability to invent and manage a story, to conduct it by means of living persons who engage the reader's interest, and to mould it, without loss of probability, into a beautiful and significant design. And this ability may be employed on material drawn from any source, on figures and incidents found in observation of daily life or purely in the poetic imagination. *Roderick Hudson* shows the genius of narrative as much as (to take an example from verse) does *Lamia*: so also does Mr. Wells's *Country of the Blind*.

It is also, of course, a power which every novelist of any merit possesses to a certain extent; and I hope it is clear that the point I have attempted to make turns on considerations of proportion and emphasis. But I think it is fair to say that until quite recently the main concern of the English novel was the display of character. Thus were produced many very admirable works; and I should be sorry if I were thought to be arguing in these tentative and far from dogmatic notes that we are now witnessing a triumph of light over darkness. I am attempting to do no more than trace what seems to be the beginning of a new movement, a new change of direction, in our literature. And it is probably fair to say as well that the novel of character tends to take as its sphere only the prose of life. The literary art (necessarily no subject for absolute definitions) can do many things: it can depict life, it can criticise life, and it can, whether on the plane of sublimity or on that of mere fantasy, create a new and substantial life of its own. But the novel in which the portrayal of character has first place over the story tends to do only the first and second of these things. It might indeed be argued that this is the proper province of the novel and that the attempt to do more invades the territory of epic or dramatic verse. But there are examples to the contrary; and at all events it is worth while for the next generation of novelists to try to prove, as I believe it will try, by further examples that the contrary is true.

It is certain that, on the whole and comparatively, the novel of character is deficient in poetic feeling and what, until criticism invents a better term, we must continue to call "atmosphere." This does not mean that the modern novel must swerve from the details of everyday life to the apparatus of romantic decoration. The squalid and sordid scenes of Mr. Conrad's *Secret Agent* are full of a poetic feeling which is not produced in Mr. Compton Mackenzie's *Carnival* or *Sinister Street* by many pages of ornamental diction and romantic

189

attitude. Nevertheless it is true that in the younger novelists something is at work which can be best, though only approximately, described as a return to the romantic. Mr. Brett Young has closer affinities with Keats or Coleridge, or, if you please, the author of *The Mysteries of Udolpho,* than with Mr. Galsworthy. Miss Romer Wilson is much nearer in spirit to Hugo or Gautier or even Goethe than to Mr. Walpole. These writers seek to free themselves from the chains of the average—which is not quite the same as the normal—and, in writing of extraordinary and interesting things, to enlarge the scope of their art.

The dangers to which the modern romanticist exposes himself are obvious enough. Mr. Brett Young's *Dark Tower* is a beautiful picture of wild and lonely country in which a strange love-story is enacted. But it is the background which remains in the reader's mind when he closes the book. The persons are too dim, their passions are too airy: they fade away and are lost in the more vivid landscape. His *Tragic Bride,* in spite of an opening of remarkable charm, poetry, and narrative skill, fails to make a complete effect because the characters are not convincing and consistent enough to support the burden of an unusual story. In Miss Wilson's latest book the chief character is conceived on lines so lofty and incredible that sometimes the author is plainly appealing to the reader to imagine for himself what her mind has conceived and her pen cannot bring forth.

The dangers of the romanticist are unreality, extravagance, absurdity, just as those of the realist are dullness and triviality. But the romanticist is attempting something different, and if he can to a reasonable extent avoid his special pitfalls he will produce something worth the risk. In his *Black Diamond*, without going outside this country or this century for his scene, Mr. Brett Young has written a picaresque novel which is a delightful and refreshing piece of work. It has proportion and symmetry, poetic feeling and loveliness of atmosphere, and, above all, rhythm and coherence of story. And Miss Wilson's *Death of Society* is a daring fantasy, which expresses beauty by means of symbols, obscure indeed yet powerful in their inarticulateness.

I have chosen these two books as illustrations of my argument because they have appeared recently. There are others. There are, in still another kind, the romances of Mr. G. K. Chesterton, *The Napoleon of Notting Hill* and *The Flying Inn*, books which may prove at some future time, in spite of the hasty negligence with which they are written (or at least the second of them), to have had more influence than is now apparent. Literature changes. One form, one attitude, is exhausted. Another appears, produces its fresh and vigorous first crops, grows exhausted in its turn, produces perhaps a crop of works which are extravagantly absurd or tediously academic. Nothing in literature is certain, not even pronouncements on books which have been in existence for centuries, still less such diagnostics and predictions as have been rashly ventured here. But this is certain, that no form of literature which ceases to develop will continue to produce good works; and, unless the novel changes, it will no longer be a living form of literature.

The Position in the Theatre

THE phrases "commercial drama" and "artistic drama" beg a good many questions and institute an offensive comparison. But they do at least correspond to a certain reality, and they indicate the existence of that strange cleavage which is the most curious feature of the modern English theatre.

The age in which we live is characteristically commercial. The word is used here in a strict, not a vaguely abusing, sense: it should convey the idea that our civilisation is more concerned with buying and selling than with production and consumption. A few human activities have succeeded in resisting the standard of values thus set up, but almost all, including the arts, have been to some extent influenced by it. If any one requires confirmation of the statement that the arts have been so influenced, let him consider the quite modern doctrine, often fanatically urged, that the artist ought to be completely indifferent to the material reward he receives for his work. Such a doctrine is clearly, in its unreason, a mere reaction against the governing principle that no human activity ought to be thought of save in terms of material reward.

In the theatre, as nowhere else in the arts, action and reaction are embodied, are recognisably separated one from the other. On the one side we have the "West End" theatres with their provincial allies, whither "West End" successes are sent on tour. On the other are such bodies as the Stage Society and the Phœnix Society, and, both in London and in the provinces, the Repertory

Theatres. The gulf is not impassable. Plays are sometimes staged in the West End for other reasons than because a manager thinks them likely to run for three hundred nights: a few can be seen which, for whatever reasons they were staged, and however they have succeeded, seem to have been written at least with an admixture of other motives. And we have all seen Repertory Theatres hastily throwing over the principle of their existence when a run of three hundred nights appeared to offer itself. But the gulf is there, and it is a gulf which is not to be found elsewhere. There are " commercial" novels and " artistic " novels; but they often come from the same publisher and sometimes from the same author. The " artistic " novel, at any rate, is not often published in a limited edition for subscribers only. No: the cleavage in the theatre is a unique thing, and the investigation of its origin and meaning leads one into the history of the English drama during the last thirty years.

For it was about thirty years ago that this phenomenon first arose. If one wanted a precise date, none better could be chosen than that of the formation of the Independent Theatre by Mr. J. T. Grein. Mr. Grein's first production was *Ghosts*; and in 1892 he produced Mr. Shaw's *Widowers' Houses*, a piece laid aside by its author seven years before because it was manifestly impossible that the ordinary stage should ever have any use for it. But the significance of the new departure escapes us if we forget what made it necessary. The English theatre, during the nineteenth century, had fallen into an almost unparalleled state of degradation. Before it reached that desert tract which somehow, parched and footsore, it yet succeeded in crossing, it

193

had always made its best writers also popular writers. Shakespeare and Jonson, Congreve and Sheridan, were not totally unsuccessful dramatists: no private subscription performances were required for *King Lear* or *Love for Love*. But in the middle of the nineteenth century there were no Shakespeares, no Sheridans. There was at best a Robertson, and below him an abysm into which it is pleasanter not to look. When the " artistic " drama was again revived it had ceased to be " commercial "; and the operation was performed by a straight and almost fanatical sect, which, with a few exceptions, has remained strait and fanatical ever since. True enough, Mr. Shaw has become an enormously successful dramatist, and Mr. Galsworthy is sometimes " put on for a run." Mr. Bennett occupies a rather ambiguous position between the two worlds, though he has not yet written the decisive play we have a right to expect from him. Mr. Somerset Maugham, who is nothing if not one of the main supports of the " commercial " drama, has written at least one comedy, *The Circle*, of surprising " artistic " quality. But the cleavage remains, deep and unmistakable.

The recapitulation of these facts may seem superfluous, for they are well known to every one who takes the slightest interest in the English theatre. But what I have called the cleavage exercises a deep influence not only on the present, but also on the future of our drama; and I do not think that any attempt, however humble and elementary, to elucidate its meaning, can be wholly in vain. It is, indeed, a somewhat surprising fact that it should still exist. When Mr. Shaw and Mr. Grein, and others, set up their standard in the 'nineties, their intention, I suppose, was to conquer or to die. They have lived and prospered, but they have not conquered. What they have achieved is the setting-up of an independent and fairly durable second state by the side of the first. The new drama, to be sure, influences its commercial brother, keeps it more or less up-to-date, and supplies it with ideas which may be converted to its own use. But it no longer hopes to drive the commercial drama from the field or even to influence it very profoundly, nor is it itself any longer in real fear of its own life. Now and again, it must be admitted, a deserving Repertory Theatre comes into the open and ululates for a millionaire to provide it with funds wherewith it may prolong its existence. I suspect, however, that commercial managements do the same almost as often, only more privately. The principal difference is that when the Repertory Theatre finds a millionaire he is called a benefactor, whereas when the commercial management finds one he is called a speculator. The chances of the two millionaires losing their money must be about even.

A contributing cause, at least, of this apathy is undoubtedly the interval caused by the war. Every person concerned, from Mr. Shaw to the youngest undergraduate, who in 1914 was reading papers on Mr. Shaw to other undergraduates, has moved on in age and nothing material has been accomplished. The old battle-cries, the old arguments, are just as valid, perhaps, as they were in 1914, but they are decidedly staler, and one revives them with a certain weariness and reluctance—a reluctance resembling that expressed in the face of a political enthusiast who at the present day hears spoken the words " Tariff Reform and Free Trade." In 1914 we were going to found a National Theatre and abolish the Censorship. In 1922 the National Theatre seems farther off than ever and the Censor has almost imperceptibly given way so much as to make it no longer worth while to pursue him, irrational as we may think his existence still to be.

But this apathy, whencever it springs, is an unnatural and unfortunate thing, and one which ought to disappear. (When I speak of apathy, I mean, of course, a certain disillusionment which prevents or weakens both propaganda and the general response to it—I do not mean to belittle the practical activities of believers in the artistic drama.) The work is by no means done, though an astonishing amount of work has been done. We have still far too few opportunities of seeing good plays; we are forced to see far too many bad ones; there are far too many discouragements put in the way of an author who wishes to write good plays.

Nevertheless, the " artistic " drama is alive and active, and needs only to be considered to have its effect. A little while after the end of the war a certain author wrote for a weekly paper a light-hearted essay on the fact that he was, now and for ever, bored with the theatre. He had had enough of what the gentleman in *Fanny's First Play* called that " played out old back number, Ibsen ": the Higher Drama and the Repertory Theatre and their supporters had got on his nerves: he wanted to hear no more about any of them ever again: as for the commercial theatre, it was not worth while eating his dinner early and struggling for a taxi to witness the trash that was presented there. These assertions caught the eye of the editor of another weekly paper, and somehow insinuated into his mind that here was the dramatic critic for whom so long and so vainly he had been searching. This editor pressed his view on our author, who, with some misgivings, accepted the post. After a few months the chief misgivings he felt were about his own earlier ideas: after a year he had passed them all under severe review and had revised many of them. He found himself still convinced that the theatre cannot live by realism alone, and must depend on it even less in the future; but he had learnt that the realist movement on which so long the " Higher Drama " has mainly depended was no negligible movement of the European mind. This little fable is designed to suggest that the staleness to which I have alluded above is largely factitious.

The " new drama," which, to some extent, all over Europe but particularly in England is definitely a recent creation, has been dominated from the first by the principle of realism. This is made not less but more obvious by the fact that the reaction against realism began almost at once, and has never until the last few years shown any signs of establishing itself. Ibsen was the first great master; and the modern movement in the theatre has never yet escaped from his influence. Of course, when we call him a realist, we must do so with innumerable reservations and qualifications. But his tendency, and even more that of his disciples, was in the direction of removing unreal conventions from the stage. Like so many literary revolutions, that which he performed was most easily obvious and most easily imitable in the matter of technique. He abolished soliloquies, and he abolished asides as well as lucky coincidences. What he presented on his stage might be life refined to an essence, but it was so refined only by careful selection,

not by any invention outside the data ordinarily
given by life. Thus he was able to present sym-
bolical and mystical conceptions in a perfectly
natural manner. *The Wild Duck* and *The Master
Builder* are far beyond being merely pictures or
even criticisms of life as it is lived (as are, for
example, *A Doll's House* and *An Enemy of the
People*), yet old Ekdal and Solness are observed
and natural persons, credible on the ordinary plane,
not creatures of the poetic imagination.

His disciples, however, adopted a sterner and
more arid form of realism. Of course, the whole
question of " realism " or " naturalism " is an
admirable subject for the process called " dis-
sociation of ideas "; and only from an intelligence
as dispassionate and patient as that of Remy de
Gourmont could we hope for an analysis of the
irrelevant details which form the common notions
designated by these terms. But realism in the
theatre meant, and still means, roughly, the adoption
of Ibsen's natural technique, the portrayal of
ordinary life as lived by large classes of the population, and, for some reason, an atmosphere of gloom
intensified to a degree which is far from realistic.
The German Naturalists considered that the artist
should paint life precisely as it is—without selection,
without purpose. Hauptmann's *Vor Sonnenaufgang*
was almost a perfect exemplification of this theory
—almost, because a perfect exemplification could
hardly survive on any stage to the last fall of the
curtain. And Mr. Galsworthy in more than one
play has reproduced scenes from ordinary life,
scenes in courts of justice or the auction-room,
exactly in every detail as they happen in ordinary
life. He even makes his characters speak exactly
the language of ordinary life—a method which
198

is said to be as heart-breaking for the actor as it is tedious for the audience.

We shall do well, however, to dismiss from consideration any definition of realism which represents it to be an aimless, unselective reproduction of everyday existence. It is only in the rarest instances that an artist can efface himself and his own sympathies without effacing also his power to interest an audience; and this applies as much to the dramatist as to any other artist. Realism consists not in reproducing reality, but in producing the illusion of reality and by that means making a comment or conveying a feeling. *A Doll's House* makes a comment: it is a criticism of society—none the less valid at this moment because Helmer's " squirrel " and " lark " need to be translated into more modern terms of endearment. But Nora and Helmer, for all that they are displayed for this purpose, are normal, credible persons; they are such persons as call on one when one moves into a new house. It is by selection and presentment that the dramatist has made them say for him what *he* desires to say. So, too, with Solness: if one has not met him, it is an accident, though what Ibsen says through him is more than a criticism on modern society. These characters, all the characters of Ibsen's later plays, exist on a different plane from the Hamlets and the Hernanis.

It was, in a sense, the corruption of the Hernanis and the Hamlets against which Ibsen and his almost unknown coadjutor, Henri Becque, and their disciples revolted. The nineteenth-century drama, especially in England, much resembled one of the characters which drama has always delighted in exploiting—the worn-out and foolish descendant of a noble race. At this moment any Londoner can see what the Elizabethan drama has come to. As I write, Sir Martin Harvey is playing in *The Only Way* at the Lyceum; and this piece, grotesque as the connection may seem, is the degenerate descendant of the great plays of blood and violence which three centuries ago pleased the London mob by their violence and their poetry. There were, in the nineteenth century, other survivals of greater days, descendants of Congreve and Sheridan and Molière, no less debased than the descendants of Shakespeare and Webster. The exponents of the new drama set their hands to the removal of all this decaying matter; and who will say that they did wrong ?

Ibsen, if it were only by his technical improvements, opened a new epoch; but that epoch was not long to endure. Perhaps it is true that realism, even in its most attenuated sense, is a spirit not very congenial to the desires of humanity: perhaps the realist method, acid and critical as it is, can never give humanity what it demands from the arts. At all events, the reaction began almost without an interval. The creations of Maeterlinck did not pretend to be real. And soon, in England, Ibsen's greatest disciple and propagandist began to develop on his own lines.

Mr. Shaw has a bifurcated personality, and consequently his own views on himself, his views expressed in the capacity of critic, are little to be trusted. He has an admirable debating brain and, when he elects to exercise it, a cool and arid intellect. But he himself has declared for " the melting moment " on the stage, and no one knows better than he how to induce the melting moment. He must be judged by his own best achievements rather than by his cooler declarations. And his own best achievements are no more realistic than Hamlet or

Coriolanus. To come no later down in his career, Cæsar and Bluntschli and Brassbound and John Tanner are pure figures of romance. No doubt the figures of an earlier romance exhibited their prowess in a different way. That remarkable survival, Cyrano de Bergerac, pinked his enemy to the tune of extremely acrobatic versifying. Mr. Shaw's heroes pink their opponents intellectually amid a shower of dazzling debating points. They are heroes of the intellect, perhaps, but they are romantic heroes none the less. They are neither conceived nor executed in a realistic attitude of mind. Mr. Shaw, it should be noted, is not, like Ibsen, an innovating genius in technique; and technique being so obvious and important, this helps to conceal the magnitude of the revolution he has effected. Ibsen's novelties were of the simple kind of which only a great revolutionary is capable. Mr. Shaw is simply one of the greatest writers for the stage that ever lived. Liszt invented no new method of using the piano; but he understood better than any other composer how to make the technical resources of the piano effective. There is no definite method of using the stage to be set to Mr. Shaw's credit; but no dramatist has ever used the scene and the actors with greater effect. He has made such dazzling use of Ibsen's reformed technique as almost to conceal the fact that he is moving in a quite contrary direction. We are too prone to judge all artists by their personal confessions; and when a dramatist, of all artists, comes into the open and proclaims his own intentions, say, in a preface, we are far too ready to rank such a declaration above the ambiguous utterances of the characters for whom he cannot be held responsible. But we must remember that an artist is more truly, though less consciously, himself in his creations than in his explanations. Despite all the admirable common sense of Mr. Shaw's prefaces, we must agree that Peter Keegan is the real man, not Larry Doyle.

Mr. Shaw's development in the direction of romanticism has been less obvious, but not less potent, than that of his great contemporary, Dr. Gerhart Hauptmann. But, while both of these writers were attached in one way or another to the original realist movement, there were younger authors who had no such attachments and whose earliest efforts were in the direction of an uncompromising revolt against realism. First among these comes Herr Hugo von Hofmannsthal, who might be described comprehensively as the greatest disappointment the modern drama has known. For Herr von Hofmannsthal, who began at an amazingly early age to write plays of great competence in very mellifluous verse, has never redeemed his too precocious promise. His *Der Abenteuerer und die Sängerin* marks the height of his powers. It has to a great degree characterisation, and a sense of the stage combined with a genuine and singular understanding of the manner in which a display of poetic eloquence can be used with dramatic effect. And this last quality is essential if, instead of proceeding from the point marked by Ibsen's reforms, we are in any manner to return to the great masters of the sixteenth and seventeenth centuries. They had an audience which appreciated poetry in its proper place. Our modern audiences seem not to appreciate poetry, but that may be because they never get it in its proper place. Herr von Hofmannsthal might have been expected to give us a lead in this direction. He took, instead, to writing librettos for Dr. Richard Strauss and to making adaptations from Sophocles, Otway, and Calderon. A certain atrophy of the creative power seems to have overtaken him. He can execute, but he can no longer conceive.

After this disappointment the question is, whether the theatre must move on Ibsen's lines and gradually expand the radius measured out by him, or whether it must take some more drastic step. And this question is not so idle and meaningless as at first sight it may seem. For the theatre is, less than any other branch of the arts, a matter of individuals. The painter and the poet may go their own ways and do what they please. The painter needs canvas and colours, the poet pen, paper, and ink: neither of them needs any more to create masterpieces. But the dramatist does need more than pen, paper, and ink: he must have a complicated organisation behind him before his masterpieces can take recognisable form. The manuscript of a novel is the novel. Whatever may prevent its publication, the work exists in final shape; and such lessons as the novelist can learn from its composition he has already learnt. But a play does not, in a proper sense, exist until it has been put on the stage by the concerted efforts of some dozen or more persons. And these dozen persons will not exert themselves unless they feel the certainty that somewhere a far larger number exists which will support them. The drama began, according to our latest theorists, in the mass feeling of the worshippers of Dionysus, or of those who worshipped the dead. The occasion of the mass feeling may have changed; its necessity remains.

We must therefore consider whether the methods of realism imposed by Ibsen and his disciples on the theatre correspond to what humanity asks from the theatre. Certainly these methods have proved to be astonishingly elastic. Mr. Shaw, that marvellous though uninventive juggler, has managed within them to write *Heartbreak House*, and Mr. Granville-Barker has managed to write *The Marrying of Anne Leete*, which remains his best, though not his most nearly perfect, play. But the methods of realism are methods devised for the presentation of the ordinary; and the fact that they can be used for other purposes does not answer the question whether other methods ought not to be devised. If I am clever enough to put a sufficiently good edge on it, I can shave with a carving-knife; but probably I should do better to buy a razor. What need have we of the conventions of the old poetic drama ?

The poetic drama does not present people as they are nor yet an illusion of people as they are. It does not give the literal transcript from reality, which is the special gift of Mr. Galsworthy, nor the abridged and modified transcript by which Ibsen creates his illusion. It shows such persons as never existed talking as no human being ever talked; and, whether they talk in verse like the persons of Webster and Shakespeare or in heavily rhythmical prose like the persons of M. Claudel, the effect is the same. They are removed from ordinary life: they are idealisations of what is important in it. Mr. Shaw, hard-driven to account for one of the characters in *Man and Superman*, said: " Every woman is not Anne, but Anne is Everywoman." It may have been a pity that he did not make Anne, and the rest of the abstractions who surrounded her, talk in verse. For verse is a method, and a method commonly understood, of proclaiming that one's representations are ideally, not literally, true to life. Thus the adoption of verse, or of some equivalent to it, is a matter of the first importance, of far more than merely technical importance. A preponderance at any time, or even a large number, of plays in verse is a certain indication that at that time realism is not the prevailing spirit.

Now, is it fanciful to suppose that a revival of the poetic drama might conquer the commercial theatre and reform it throughout as the drama of Ibsen has failed to do? We have seen that the revolution of the nineties was successful in so far as it established a secure place for itself. It did so much because it appealed immediately to intelligent persons who liked the theatre, but were driven away from it by the corruption of greater days, which was all that they could find there. Yet it remained strictly unpopular; and does not one feel, with the art of the drama, that what is unpopular is proportionately unsatisfactory? And is this not because its realistic basis, which the new drama has often transcended but never forgotten, is too narrow for genuine public appreciation? Is the modern public quite incapable of appreciating good art in the theatre, or is it merely not moved by the particular form of good art at present offered to it? In this connection we ought to observe that among those productions which have recently attained, by more or less common consent, both artistic and commercial success are *The Beggar's Opera* and the Russian Ballet. These have received popular support in a measure denied to works which have been, perhaps, equally good, but in a different way.

Of the possibilities and probabilities of such an extensive movement there is at present little to say. Verse is not an essential, though it is hard not to believe that were a revival of the essentially poetic drama to take place it would not bring verse with it. But verse has its drawbacks as well as its merits. Our common dramatic blank verse is haunted. For a long time hardly any one has been able to use it without producing a million reverberating echoes which blurr what he himself has to say; and no one has yet evolved any formal rhythm which can satisfactorily take its place.

But speculations on such details as these are, no doubt, out of place and unprofitable. What we have to consider is whether the " artistic " drama was not limited at the outset in its range and its appeal by the circumstances in which it received its new life; whether it is not, in virtue of these limitations, a thing only for the few, not a thing which only a few as yet enjoy, though all should do so.

Folk-Song as Poetry

THE great mass of folk poetry in the English language, with the exception of the Scottish and Border ballads and the Scottish songs rehandled by Burns, has been rescued only during the last twenty years or so from a fast-decaying oral tradition. The work of collection has been carried out almost entirely by musicians, who have found the verses in a highly corrupt state and have accepted the corruption with a regret that is soon assuaged by the extreme beauty of the tunes. Mr. Cecil Sharp has been the most industrious worker in the musical field, and his judgment on the poetic side of the subject is expressed in one sentence in his excellent book, *English Folk Song: Some Conclusions*. "The truth is," he says, in his brief chapter on folk-poetry, "that the twentieth century collector is a hundred years too late." It is plain that he expects no answer to his final question: "Who will do for our English ballads and songs what Scott and Burns did for the Scottish?" But if it is not likely that any one can ever do so much as this, it is still possible that the few pieces of unspoilt folk-song that are left may come into English poetry as an enlivening and simplifying influence.

If this does happen, it will be to the musicians and in a very high degree to Mr. Sharp that we shall owe it; and now more than ever, since he has added to his exhaustive collection of Somerset songs a new and very rich collection from America.[1] It

[1] *English Folksongs from the Southern Appalachians.* Collected by Oliver Dame Campbell and Cecil J. Sharp. (Putnam.)

207

First Essays on Literature

has long been known that certain English ballads
survived in the United States, and *The Hangman's
Tree*, a version of *The Maid Freed from the Gallows*,
sung in Virginia with traces of Yorkshire dialect,
has often been quoted as the classical example.
But Mrs. Campbell and Mr. Sharp have done more
than discover a few isolated survivals. His introduction to their book transcends its purpose and
reads like a narrative of the discovery of the Earthly
Paradise, or one of those adventure-stories in which
lucky hunters stumble on a secluded abundance of
rare game. The mountain country which they
explored extends from the borders of Pennsylvania
half-way into Alabama, is bounded roughly by the
thousand-feet contour line, and contains some
three million inhabitants, exclusive of city-dwellers.
The district is inaccessible, and it is in consequence
largely unspoilt. Its inhabitants are economically
independent, their wants are few, they do not
produce for sale, and therefore they have much
leisure and a highly developed social sense. It is
obvious that Mr. Sharp thought himself in a sort
of Earthly Paradise; and indeed he cannot prevent
a certain note of the fabulous from creeping into his
description. " I found myself," he says, " for the
first time in my life in a community in which singing
was as common and almost as universal a practice
as speaking." And the following passage would
sound more at home in *Utopia* or *Erewhon* or
Morris's *Nowhere* than in the United States:—

" They have an easy unaffected bearing and
the unselfconscious manners of the well-bred. I
have received salutations upon introduction or on
bidding farewell, dignified and restrained, such as
a courtier might make to his Sovereign. Our work

208

naturally led to the making of many acquaintances, and, in not a few cases, to the formation of friendships of a more intimate nature, but on no single occasion did we receive anything but courtesy and friendly treatment. Strangers that we met in the course of our long walks would usually bow, doff the hat, and extend the hand, saying, ' My name is ——; what is yours ? ' an introduction which often led to a pleasant talk and sometimes to singing and the noting of interesting ballads."

In this wonderland Mr. Sharp and Mrs. Campbell collected in nine weeks without any difficulty the astonishing number of 122 songs and ballads and 323 tunes. It is no surprise after this to learn that they have not yet done with the Appalachians. Many of the melodies here printed are new and of great beauty and interest; but I am not at present concerned with them. Many of the verses are also new, but most of them are unfortunately as corrupt as the English songs. In a number of pieces there are references to London and " bonny Scotland " that have survived the Atlantic passage; but there are also traces of American environment. Thus *Lord Rendal*, who appears as a noble and tragic figure in the best English versions, figures in the Appalachians as *Jimmy Randolph*, and declares that he will leave to his father, in one version, " my horses, my buggies, mother," and in another " my mules and wagons," while one song represents his fatal meal to have been " cold pie and cold coffee " —these words being sung to a musical phrase which is really exquisitely touching. But in spite of variations of this kind, the general tone, manner, and diction of the songs are identical with those collected in England, and make a valuable addition to them for the present purpose of guessing at the real poetic value of folk-song in spite of its dilapidation.

It is an excellent feature in this book that the number of songs given exceeds the number of ballads—by more, indeed, than the actual classification shows, for some of those given as ballads would obviously come more justly under the heading of songs. The effect of the influence of ballads on literary poetry is often to produce " fakes " of varying merit; but the influence of " folk " songs, a later and more personal development, has generally produced, in the few cases in which it has been exercised, a fresher and simpler form of lyrical expression. Unfortunately, in the Appalachians, as in England, the songs are rather more degraded than the ballads, possibly because they have no fixed narratives to keep tradition in the straight line. But there are here and there flashes of lyrical beauty, from which it is possible to divine what was the excellence of this poetry when it was in the comparatively pure state of the ballads collected by Percy and Scott. Mr. Sharp calls attention to the poetic merit of some of these songs, and his literary judgment is certainly not at fault. He quotes one really touching verse:—

" When I see your babe a-laughing,
    It makes me think of your sweet face;
But when I see your babe a-crying,
    It makes me think of my disgrace."

And three more, from another piece, in which the quaintnesses are inessential and the lyric feeling of the highest excellence:—

" When your heart was mine, true love,
    And your head lay on my breast,
You could make me believe by the falling of
      your arm
    That the sun rose up in the west.

There's many a girl can go all round about
    And hear the small birds sing,
And many a girl that stays at home alone
    And rocks the cradle and spin.

There's many a star that shall jingle in the west,
    There's many a leaf below,
There's many a damn will light upon a man
    For serving a poor girl so."

The assumption that the songs are of later origin
than the ballads is, of course, only an assumption;
but it would be easy to defend it by *a priori* arguments. It seems natural to suppose that their
personal character springs from a more self-conscious stage of development; and, whatever may
be the case with the ballads, I cannot bring myself
to believe that the songs are not of individual
authorship.[1] This supposition takes away from
one section of folk-poetry, at least, the mysterious
and quasi-magical attributes with which some of
its admirers have invested it, and puts it into its
proper place in the development of English verse.
I can see no difficulty in believing that there existed
during the height of the Middle Ages, and later,
generations of lyricists who remained anonymous

---

[1] I cannot now bring myself to believe that the ballads were
composed otherwise than by individuals. But it seems fair to say
that the song-writers were more conscious of their separate artistic
individualities than the ballad-writers.

merely because opportunities for named authorship
did not exist. These lyricists were diverted from
oral tradition to print by a purely mechanical cause
in the Elizabethan age; and they were simultaneously influenced by the "literary" poetry
already practised in Provence, Italy, and France.
But they did not all leave anonymity; nor did they
all lose the folk-song tone. There are many Elizabethan pieces, such as *Greensleeves* and Nashe's
songs, which hesitate on the "imaginary line"
between "literary" and "popular" poetry. There
is at least one verse in this book—

> "Awake! awake! you drowsy sleeper,
>   Awake! awake! it's almost day;
> How can you lie and sleep and slumber
>   And your true love going far away?"

—which has a distinctly Elizabethan ring about
it. It is a tenable theory that the extraordinary
freshness, vigour and brilliance of Elizabethan
song-writing may have been a result of the first
mingling of the "literary" with the "popular"
manner, producing in a whole generation of poets
an effect somewhat similar to that which was produced in Germany in the eighteenth century by a
similar cause.

Let it be assumed then that the fragments which
the musical collectors have rescued represent a body
of fine poetry, fairly comparable with that of
Elizabethan song-writers. What is the task which
would confront the modern Burns or Scott whose
assistance Mr. Sharp so despairingly invokes? His
task would be, I am afraid, impossible. He would
find exquisite stanzas afloat in the most incongruous
surroundings, such as the "Cuckoo" verse, which

appears constantly without any particular relevance
to its context:—

> " The cuckoo is a fine bird
>   He sings as he flies,
> He brings us good tidings
>   And he tells us no lies.
> He sucks the sweet flowers
>   To make his voice clear,
> And the more he sings ' Cuckoo '
>   The summer draws near."

He would also find stanzas beginning finely with:—

> " The ripest apple's soonest rotten,"

and ending in flat corruption with:—

> " As by experience it is known."

He would find whole pieces which are almost
perfect, such as *The Unquiet Grave*, which begins:—

> " Cold blows the wind to my true love,
>   And gently drops the rain.
> I never had but one sweetheart
>   And in greenwood she lies slain,"

and continues on the same level to the end.   He
would also find pieces which are throughout on the
level of—

> " I stayed away six weeks
>   And it caused her to complain.
> She wrote me a letter saying:
>   Come back again,
>   O come back again,"

and in which the thing he would be searching for would still be faintly and maddeningly perceptible. Out of these elements it would be his business to make a body of poetry equal in excellence and betraying nowhere the touch of the sophisticated literary versifier. An impossible task! But it may still be possible, by very careful editing, to produce a collection which will give an impression of what might have been; and the sooner this task is undertaken the better. It would involve considerable labour and trouble, for the principal collections are in manuscript; but I am convinced that it would reward the enthusiast, and not only enlarge the stock of poetic beauty, but also exercise an admirable influence on contemporary and future poetry. The devoted editor must be a man free from all antiquarian and scientific preoccupations, and he must also have a certain amount of courage; for the most maddening thing that the modern emulant of Burns will find is that all the printed collections of folk-song are mercilessly bowdlerised.

The Sonnets and Common Sense

In spite of Browning's protest, the world of persons interested in such things continues to believe with Wordsworth that Shakespeare unlocked his heart in the sonnets; and, not only do they accept this view, but they seem to consider that there is hardly any other way in which the sonnets can be regarded. Mr. Knox Pooler, the editor of the new *Arden* edition, is not a fanatic, and is not wedded to any particular theory; but he clearly thinks that this is the principal matter to be treated in any discussion of the works; and, after analysing the value of Benson's edition of 1640 with this problem chiefly in mind, he proceeds to outline the various explanations that have been offered by speculators. And this is indeed the point to which most readers will first turn, even those who feel in the midst of their curiosity, that they are displaying something less than a proper sense of the dignity of literature. For the lack of information and the plethora of hints combine to make what we know of Shakespeare's life rather like a detective story from which the last chapter is missing.

Nothing can be plainer than that the full tale of Shakespeare's life would be more exciting than the life of, say, Crabbe. At some time, somehow, the man who wrote the sonnets and the plays found himself involved in an emotional predicament, of which the sonnets are the expression. The baffling dedication cannot be dismissed, but must conceal a real meaning. So must the famous line in Sonnet XX.:—

" A man in hew all *Hews* in his controlling."

The italics alone require explanation, though neither they nor the purport of the line necessitate the hypothesis that the sonnets were addressed to a youth named Hughes. His name may have been Rose, a word italicised, equally inexplicably, in the second line of Sonnet I. But there is besides these a multitude of hints and clues scattered throughout the sonnets, all of which are meaningless from the literary point of view. And it is only human in us that we should want to know the story pointed at by these clues. It is absurd to dismiss all demand for biographical detail as appetite for more " chatter about Harriet "—peculiarly absurd in that this demand is deprecated only when it is applied to the lives of artists. It is not thought unworthy, for example, that we should seek for evidence of Napoleon's personality elsewhere than in his campaigns and statesmanship; and there is no reason why we should not desire to study the characters of great poets in their private lives exactly as we study other natural phenomena.

But it is a mistake to imagine, because there is a story and because we want to know it, that there is necessarily any hope of knowing it. The mistake of the critics has been, not so much that they sought in the sonnets information rather than exaltation, as that they examined them in a way more proper to the examination of affidavits than to that of personal poetry. This is not merely a mistaken, but also a necessarily sterile, mode of procedure. The sonnets are not a precise summary of facts; they have this in common with most other poetry, that they are made up of exceedingly imprecise allusions to facts. The direct statements made in them carry the inquirer nowhere; and attempted interpretations of them may carry him anywhere. It might be argued, for example, that in the opening series, in which Shakespeare ostensibly urges his friend to marry, he is really exhorting a young man—possibly a noble—not to despise, but to use his own talents. It is impossible to assert that Shakespeare could not have used this disguise for this purpose. It is equally impossible to prove that he did so use it, or even to give the hypothesis any primacy among others. A moment's reflection on any personal poetry as to the origins of which we have fuller information will show the impossibility of reaching certitude from the text alone. What should we make of Shelley's connection with Emilia Viviani, if we had no better witness than *Epipsychidion* and its preface? And even in the case of that confessed autobiographer Goethe, the lyrics and *Werther* would give us a very incorrect impression of the events of his youth.

Another moment's consideration devoted to the clues on which all theories are based will show what an insubstantial foundation they make for either positive or negative conclusions. The fact that Shakespeare spoke of " the proud, full sail " of some one's " great verse " indicates at most that Shakespeare considered some poet worthy of the phrase, or, at least, that its inappropriateness was not sufficient to trouble about. If he had had Drayton in mind, the standard of his criticism would have been no worse than that of some other great poets. On the other hand, Mr. Knox Pooler thinks the lines in Sonnet LXXXVI.:—

> " . . . That affable familiar ghost
> Which nightly gulls him with intelligence,"

too slender evidence to establish an allusion to Chapman's *Shadow of Night*. But the connection may have been perfectly obvious to the recipient of the sonnets if there had been jesting between him and Shakespeare on this subject. But the point of the whole matter is that, as every one knows who stops to think, poetry of this sort is not written with a view to making the details of a situation clear to outsiders. When Shakespeare had expressed his emotions, taking care, perhaps (but perhaps not), to do so in a way intelligible to the two other persons immediately concerned, he was satisfied. A poem, when all is said and done, is a poem and not an affidavit.

And the sonnets are poems. That appears in the end to be the only profitable angle from which to view them, whether for enjoyment or for investigation. It is true that this method will not disclose the name of the mistress or the friend; but it is the only way to arrive at an understanding of the emotional situation out of which the sequence arose; and this, with the light which it throws on Shakespeare's poetic, and on his merely human, character, is perhaps after all the thing most to be desired. The sonnets are undoubtedly as characteristic a work of Shakespeare as any other. They are as superior to the sonnets of the time as his plays are to other plays. And they contain, as it were, a compendium of Shakespeare's gifts. In them it is possible to parallel the pure poetry of the plays, the lines in which the dramatist stands free of human relationships, whether real or invented, and surveys life and nature from a general standpoint. Such lines as:—

". . . Daffodils
That come before the swallow dares and take
The winds of March with beauty,"

may be compared with:—

. . Those boughs which shake against the
    cold,
Bare ruined choirs, where late the sweet birds
    sang."

But it is also impossible in the sonnets to equal the snatches of dramatic intensity, fiery sentences pulled out of particular events and persons, in which the plays abound. The sonnet beginning:—

" When my love swears that she is made of truth,
    I do believe her, though I know she lies,"

is as full of passion, of particular life, as Othello's cry:—

". . . Thou weed
That art so lovely fair and smell'st so sweet,
That the sense aches at thee."

But the distinction which emerges here and which may be very roughly and imperfectly defined as the difference between *general* or *ideal* and *particular* or *personal* poetry may, perhaps, throw a clearer light on the meaning of the sonnets than any inquiry into clues and allusions.

For the *particular* poetry, the utterance of immediate personal feeling, occurs with much greater frequency in the few sonnets in which the dark lady is concerned than in the more numerous sonnets addressed to the friend. An examination of the two groups reveals a disparity of tone, which is easier to distinguish than to demonstrate or to define. Such sonnets as :—

" When I consider everything that grows
Holds in perfection but a little moment,"

contain, it is true, each a universal reflection and a particular application; but the reader cannot avoid feeling that the universal reflection is in each case the heart and motive of the piece. These are poems, not on the beauty of Shakespeare's friend, but on beauty, not on Shakespeare's separation from his friend, but on separation, not on a particular friendship, but on friendship. But when Shakespeare wrote on his mistress, the particular woman, the emotion of the moment absorbed him. These sonnets are direct cries of passion; but the passion of the sonnets to the friend is born of the contemplation of life as a whole.

This is not meant to imply that Shakespeare's friendship was a fictitious thing, merely an excuse for poetry. The sonnets suggest far more that it was an attachment in the fashion of the time, sincere so far as it went, but not going much further than the adoption of a pleasing young man as an object for an ideal devotion analogous to that which Tuscan poets felt for their ladies. It was this devotion, perhaps somewhat frigid and artificial, which, as it were, served to set free the results of Shakespeare's passionate contemplation of life. His attachment to the dark lady was obviously, from the sonnets in which she appears, a matter which touched him personally in a far more poignant way. The collision between the two attachments, which is the climax of the sonnets, makes a moving situation. It is the clash between devotion to an idea and passion for a human being realised in the strictest and most difficult terms. And—though perhaps this is due to feeble humanity, which always thinks that a devil is a more realistic creation than an angel—it seems possible even here to find a distinction between the ideal devotion and the fleshly passion, which run side by side, as the water of a muddy tributary is sometimes clearly visible long after it has joined a more limpid stream.

These are no doubt sufficiently inexact attempts at exactitude in definition of a situation which Shakespeare might have found it difficult briefly or even consistently to define. It must be remembered that the position and feelings of the protagonists must have changed from day to day, and consequently from sonnet to sonnet; for it is most unlikely that the whole sequence was written as a set work when the affair was closed. There is no retrospective tinge in the more personal sonnets. But perhaps enough has been said to suggest that the consideration of style is a better avenue by which to approach the problem than the detective method commonly employed, which has yielded as many theories as there are sonnets and still offers no hope of giving any one theory a definite lead over all its rivals.

Shelley as a Lyric Poet

PROFESSOR HERFORD, in his introduction to this beautiful volume,[1] makes out a good case for abandoning Mrs. Shelley's division of her husband's works into "principal" and "miscellaneous" poems. He remarks that it is hard to understand why later editors should have given the rank of a "principal" poem to the *Letter to Maria Gisborne* and denied it to *The Sensitive Plant*. He contends that Shelley's verse is best displayed when it is grouped according to kinds, that *Epipsychidion* and *Adonais* glow brightest when close to the shorter lyrics, and that *The Revolt of Islam* and *Alastor* gain lustre by keeping company. He gives therefore in the present volume all the poems which he considers lyrical, followed by all the translations, and he reserves for three further volumes the epic and narrative poetry, the dramatic poetry and the juvenilia.

His theory is plausible, and its plausibility is much increased by the fact that *Epipsychidion* does shine more gloriously in its chronological place among *The Cloud*, the *Epithalamium* and *The Recollection*. But if a reader who knows Shelley well allows himself to drift once or twice through this book, forming his impressions into a clear picture, he will soon become aware that he is regarding, not a particular facet of Shelley's genius, but the whole of it in epitome. He will be hard put to it to name any peculiar Shelleyan quality

---

[1] *The Lyrical Poems and Translations of Percy Bysshe Shelley.* Arranged in Chronological Order, with a Preface by C. H. Herford. Florence Press Edition. (Chatto and Windus.)

which is discoverable in the rest of the poet's works
and not here.   And the deduction to be drawn
from this fact is fairly obvious.   Shelley's genius is
(except in *The Cenci* and one or two poems of much
less note) purely lyrical.   There is no perceptible
difference between the *Epithalamium* or the *Ode
to Heaven* and a hundred or more passages from
Prometheus Unbound or *Hellas*.   Who could tell, on
grounds of style and feeling alone, whether

" I cannot tell my joy when o'er a lake
   Upon a drooping bough with nightshade twined
   I saw two azure halcyons clinging downward
   And thinning one bright bunch of amber berries,
   With quick long beaks and in the deep there lay
   Those lovely forms imaged as in a sky; "

and

" I am drunk with the honey wine
   Of the moon-unfolded eglantine,
   Which fairies catch in hyacinth bowls; "

and

" Like loveliness panting with wild desire
   While it trembles with fear and delight,
   Hesperus flies from awakening night,
   And pants in its beauty and speed with light
   Fast-flashing, soft, and bright; "

and

" A ship is floating in the harbour now,
   A wind is hovering o'er the mountain's brow;
   There is a path on the sea's azure floor,
   No keel has ever ploughed that path before;
   The halcyons brood around the foamless isles;
   The treacherous Ocean has forsworn its wiles;
   The merry mariners are bold and free "

—who could tell whether these passages should be placed, in accordance with Professor Herford's principle of division, among lyrical or narrative or dramatic poems ? The same movement animates each of them. They are all lyrical in spirit; and the vast bulk of Shelley's work is created by a purely lyrical impulse. Professor Herford half confesses this when he includes all the fragments in this volume. Some of these are undoubtedly intended for poems which were to have been dramatic or narrative in form; but it is quite impossible to assign them to their categories, and they all have the lyrical characteristic in common.

The lyric is the most spontaneous and therefore the most inexplicable form of poetry. We speak a little too often, perhaps, of the " lyrical cry "; but it is of all forms of composition the nearest to an exclamation, the form in which evidence of artifice is most destructive. A lyric should have the power which passion throws into an instinctive glance or gesture; and instinctive action is that which criticism, whether of conduct or letters, finds hardest to analyse. But certain distinctions may be made according to the character of the lyricist. If it be true that Keats wrote poetry with his senses and Wordsworth with his conscience, then it is also true that Shelley wrote poetry with his nerves. His nerves, so far as we can fumblingly associate poetic qualities with physical condition, made him what he was. Many commentators have been puzzled by Shelley's sicknesses and his own opinions regarding them. As a very young man, he thought himself attacked by phthisis, gave himself up for lost, and recovered with startling rapidity and unconcern. He was troubled later by mysterious complaints, attacks of pain, lassitude, and des-

pondency, for which even he could offer no explanation intelligible in the medical language of his
time.   But the explanation is sufficiently simple.
He suffered from neurasthenia; and this is now
recognised to be a definite disease, as little and
as much within the control of the patient as almost
all other diseases.   It accounts for his symptoms, the
physical pains which revealed nothing and led to
nothing, the rapid alternations between high excitement and dejected despair, the delusions and
hallucinations to which he was subject.   It does not,
of course, wholly account for his adventures of the
heart.   But much too much rubbish has been written
on this aspect of his life, both by accusers and
defenders.   It is absurd to suggest, as Matthew
Arnold suggests, that his extreme susceptibility
in this direction was something altogether abnormal.
Equals in inflammability could be found in any
street in any town; and from most of these Shelley
is distinguished only by his seriousness and by his
lack of that sense of humour which generally checks
the first promptings of the spirit and helps to
preserve social balance.   We all have too many
unconfessable follies of the mind to remember for
any one of us to regard Shelley as a separated man
merely because he carried a few lesser wildnesses
into action.

He was abnormal, or more accurately, unusual,
in so far as he was a poet; and he may be distinguished among poets by the extent to which
nervous excitement can be traced as the moving
impulse of his work.   Some critics have decided
that it is derogatory to the dignity of poetry to
ascribe it to the action of disease.   It would certainly be disgusting to think that the germs of
tuberculosis *caused* genius in Keats; but this was

First Essays on Literature

a malignant disease, a mere rotting away and
corruption of the body, a thing in itself repulsive.
We do not equal Shelley's poetry with the pearl
in the oyster if we say that it and his neurasthenia
were alike products of the especial delicacy and
sensibility of his perceptions. The impressions
which life made on him resulted now in nervous
derangement and now in sublime poetry. His
inspiration was much more like the madness which,
in popular opinion, alone deserves the name, than
that which visits most poets. It very closely
resembled—for we should as far as possible connect
the phenomena of poetry with the ordinary phenomena of intuition and expression—that feeling of
speed and lightness of thought which accompany
any strong mental excitement induced by vigorous
conversation or a new and stimulating train of
ideas.

Speed and lightness are the images which
dominate Shelley's poetry. Alastor

> " Felt the boat speed o'er the tranquil sea
> Like a torn cloud before the hurricane."

In the first canto of *The Revolt of Islam*:—

> " Swift and swifter grew the vessel's motion,
> So that a dizzy trance fell on my brain."

The Witch of Atlas breathed " the soul of swiftness "
into her boat, and in the glorious last stanza of
Adonais the image of the flying vessel recurs in
perhaps its most significant form. But this image
is not the only instance of Shelley's obsession with
rapidity. Desire, for him, has " lightning feet ";
the coursers of the Chariot of the Hours " are fed
with lightning, they drink of the whirlwind's

226

stream." The *Ode to the West Wind* and *The Cloud* are both written of swift things, and are full of their swiftness: the *Skylark* renders the rapidity both of the bird's soaring and of its song. When Shelley said that peace was less often seen in his mind than calm in waters, he meant, though he may not have known it, that the waters of his mind were always troubled by the rush of vivid and poignant sensations to which his nervous constitution laid him open.

The ease and light motion of his verse may have something to do with the creation of this impression in the reader's mind; but it would probably be more accurate to say that he shaped for himself a quickly moving medium to carry the rapidity of his thought and feeling. Both feeling and versification are displayed at their finest in *Epipsychidion* and *Adonais*, neither of which is long enough to allow the reader to be bewildered by the flow of images, and in *Prometheus Unbound* and *Hellas*, where the action divides the headlong rush of the verse enough to make it comprehensible. But the impossibility of arranging Shelley's work according to forms is demonstrated by *The Revolt of Islam*, an epic written in an almost entirely lyrical spirit. It can hardly be said that, in any given passage of this composition of nearly five thousand lines, the poet falls signally below the average of his mature work; but the epic is nevertheless a tremendous failure. The cantos whirl by so fast that it becomes impossible to distinguish individual images and incidents; the flashes of beauty dazzle the eye and ruin the poem by their own abundance and lack of submission to any ordered scheme. Shelley himself is partly bewildered by his own swiftness, and the reader is totally overwhelmed. It is an epic written by a

227

poet whose genius was wholly lyrical; and there could be no better proof of the strength of his lyrical genius than that, in such a form as this, it should have wrecked the mould into which it was poured and have still preserved in a recognisable condition its own misused loveliness and ardency. In *The Cenci* alone Shelley stays his flight and moves at the proper pace of tragedy; but this piece is admittedly an exceptional *tour de force.* It would be, if Professor Herford were to base his arrangement on spirit rather than on form, almost the only piece to be placed in the section devoted to non-lyrical poems.

Keats and his Critics

MATTHEW ARNOLD spoke of " the admirers whose pawing and fondness does not good, but harm, to the fame of Keats; who concentrate attention upon what in him is least wholesome and most questionable." But Sir Sidney Colvin is not one of these. His truly exhaustive biography [1] seems to have been designed partly as ballast that will for ever prevent the poet's reputation from rising unsteadily into the skies of romance. But it is not merely exhaustive. It is written in a lively and genial fashion; it is copiously illustrated with extracts from Keats's own poems and letters and from such writings of others as throw any light on him; and it presents a picture, neither diminished nor exaggerated, both of his life and of the progress of his fame. It is not particularly original. No new material has been found which can be used to contradict the generally accepted story; and Sir Sidney Colvin's critical judgments are sound but not revolutionary. But in one important particular he has followed the traditional reading, where a different interpretation of the evidence might have lead him to give a very different cast to his tale.

He repeats, that is to say, the old fallacy that Keats was somehow peculiarly unfortunate in the criticism and recognition of his work; and while he denies that *Blackwood* and the *Quarterly* were causes of the poet's death, he ascribes to their

[1] *John Keats, His Life and Poetry, His Friends, Critics, and After-Fame.* By Sidney Colvin. (Macmillan.)

opinion consequences that embittered his last days and would have ruined his career. He implies that Keats might reasonably have expected treatment of a very different sort. This reveals a certain tendency to forget the real world in which we live, to construct an ideal dwelling-place for his hero, and to treat as outrageous events in that conventional universe things which are the commonplaces of ordinary life. There is no particular reason why Sir Sidney Colvin should set up for Keats's generation an ideal standard of conduct which he would not apply to his own; and his apparent expectation that all reviewers should be at all times singularly discerning and singularly conscientious is really rather absurd.

Keats had, as a matter of fact, a fate which some living poets might feel disposed to envy. It is more necessary than ever, in view of this volume, to emphasise the facts that he was not yet twenty-six when he died, and that his last line was written before he was twenty-five. Yet with his first two, very immature books, he became a battle-cry and the subject of contention between hostile parties. Had he lived to-day he would have received, like Flecker, " an insolent ten-line review with a batch of nincompoops "; and such praise as was given him would have been as cautious as Leigh Hunt's was bold. The virulence of the attacks made on him was the complement of the enthusiasm with which his friends encouraged him. We are less vivid to-day in our literary passions; and the equability of mind which forbids us to see in poetry anything very provocative, whether for praise or blame, is not necessarily an advance on the era of Lockhart and Jefferies.

There is no evidence that Keats was much more

disturbed by the venom of *Blackwood's* than he would have been to-day if some paper had warned him in small type, with complete accuracy, that he was taking dangerous liberties with the English language. Certainly Lockhart's invective was more than ordinarily scurrilous, but it was couched in the dialect of the time. Keats himself writes: " I have no cause to complain, because I am certain anything really fine will in these days be felt." He says again that " the attempt to crush me in the *Quarterly* has only brought me more into notice "; and Reynolds fully expresses the true significance of the whole affair when he assures his friend that men do not set their muscles and strain their sinews to break a straw." Croker and Lockhart (setting aside for a moment their political prejudice) were vaguely and unconsciously disturbed by those virtues in Keats which presaged a development of poetry strange and unfriendly to them; and they fell upon his obvious faults with relief. This, of course, is not meant to excuse the person whom Mr. Buxton Forman delighted to describe as " the noteless blot." The fact that contemporary fashion partly explains the violence of Keats's enemies ought not to prevent us from stigmatising bad criticism when we see it, or from denouncing the intellectual fault, even less pardonable than their æsthetic blindness, which led them to attack his poetry because they disliked his politics. But there is no trace of jealousy, which is the only quite unpardonable motive for severe criticism; and they may be acquitted with fair certainty of having done any positive harm to his health or to his career.

The most illuminating contribution made by Sir Sidney Colvin to this discussion is his memory of Andrew Lang " wondering whether in like circumstances he might not have himself committed a like offence, and with no *Hyperion* or *St. Agnes' Eve*, or *Odes* yet written, and only the 1817 volume and *Endymion* before him, have dismissed Keats fastidiously and scoffingly." It is not impossible that he should have done so; and those who dare affirm of themselves the contrary must have greater faith in their own powers of discernment than the practice of criticism commonly generates. Let us own that the adverse critics attacked Keats more for his faults than for his virtues; the charge against them is that they judged by too narrow a standard and did not allow his virtues to plead sufficiently in extenuation. But the faults in his early work are admitted to-day, even by his warmest admirers, to be of a very glaring and disagreeable sort. The publication of his first book was an act of folly; the publication of a first book often is. *Endymion* was in some respects not ripe for print; and even Arnold wished it away from Keats's works. Keats himself condemned it in his Preface; and though, as Sir Sidney remarks, this Preface should, by its tone, have saved him from savagery, yet it is hard to reproach severely the critics who reinforced the author's own charges of mawkishness and feverishness.

I do not think that enough consideration has been given to the question whether " the noteless blot " may not have had some hand in the supreme excellence of his victim's later work. There are some poets on whom unsympathetic criticism has only a crushing or a withering effect; but I do not find it easy to reckon Keats among this number. His great sensitiveness and the weakness produced by disease at the end of his life have rather obscured for us his courage and the resilience of his temperament. But if we admit, as I think we must, that his enemies did no real injury either to his health or his prospects, we may be content to look for what benefits they may have conferred on him by their castigation of his style. He was—let me say again—very young and, with all his sturdiness of character, both volatile and impressionable. He was beginning to be a little repelled by Hunt's personality; and he may have been disposed to assent to the strictures drawn on him by the tricks of style he had learnt from Hunt. The faults for which he was chastised were mainly faults of indiscipline; and the note of his letters during this time is his determination to discipline himself and to compose with complete artistic self-consciousness. Only a few months afterwards he wrote the first of the odes, the *Psyche*, and said that it was " the first and only poem with which I have taken even moderate pains "; but nearly all that he did afterwards was done with pains, and showed him freeing himself by a conscious effort from his faults of mawkishness and affectation. His third volume produced—as it might well have done—a real chorus of praise; and only the sudden disaster which overtook him prevented him from beginning a career of prosperity and fame at the age of twenty-five.

He was really the wonderful youth of poetry, for Chatterton and Rimbaud may be better described as miraculous boys. There is nothing in the history of literature like the youth of Keats unless it be the youth of Goethe; and it is not altogether fanciful to imagine that Keats's career, had it been prolonged, might have surpassed that of the German poet. Both were eclipsed for a time by a school of false taste and implicated in circles of mawkish and effeminate persons. Both experienced a wonderful release; and there is a certain similarity in freshness and beauty between the poems of the 1820 volume and the songs which Goethe wrote for Friederike Brion. Keats, however, had a fundamental strain of melancholy with which Goethe's developed despair does not offer a true comparison. But the daring and lofty reach of Goethe's *Prometheus* may be paralleled by the determination which Keats expressed in the second version of *Hyperion* to be one of those

> " Who love their fellows even to the death,
> Who feel the giant agony of the world,
> And more, like slaves to poor humanity,
> Labour for mortal good."

It would be dangerous to press the comparison too far. It breaks down chronologically, and it is, like all such comparisons, useful only in that it points towards a conclusion which can be more substantially supported. It suggests, that is to say, that Keats might have become a poet in whom the intellectual and moral would have balanced and controlled the sensual and emotional faculties.

Intellectual power is comparatively rare in modern poets. Shakespeare and Milton had it, and Wordsworth, though in him it was not always so well sustained by other qualities. It was subjected in Shelley to a certain warping that, up to his death, deprived it of some of its value. Keats was gifted with a full and rich sensuous nature, and this was the quality chiefly displayed in his best work.

Lamia is no more than a picture exquisitely done, *St. Agnes' Eve* a vivid impression of a dramatic situation, the *Nightingale* the expression of a mood. The *Grecian Urn*, striving to express a philosophic truth, does not quite unify it with the poetry; and the *Melancholy*, which succeeds better in this way, does not stand, absolutely considered, among his very finest pieces.

But the revised *Hyperion*, as Mr. Bridges long ago pointed out—though Sir Sidney Colvin does not wholly agree with him—is not a deterioration, but a first, necessarily imperfect, attempt at a much grander manner. And the poetry towards which it points, with its tragic incompletion, is a poetry which is philosophical in character. Philosophical poetry is no more merely the enunciation of philosophical propositions in verse than sensual poetry is the enumeration of sensual pleasures in verse; it must be the expression of a temperament which is at once inherently poetical and philosophical We know that Keats was poetical; no statement could be less in need of demonstration. And the indication from the revised *Hyperion* that his nature was inherently philosophical can be supported by a hundred passages from his letters—not so much those that record his mental discoveries as those which betray his temper and the cast of his mind. Arnold quotes one as a proof of character:—

" I know nothing, I have read nothing; and I mean to follow Solomon's directions: ' Get learning get understanding.' There is but one way for me. The road lies through application, study, and thought. I will pursue it."

That is not merely the exclamation of a seriously

minded man; it is the resolution of a poet ambitious enough for his poetry to be determined to base it nobly on a foundation of real wisdom. And elsewhere he shows not only the right humble and hopeful attitude to life, but a step towards the imaginative appreciation of it:—

" Though I am myself pursuing the same instinctive course as the veriest human animal you can think of, I am, however young, writing at random, straining at particles of light in the midst of a great darkness, without knowing the bearing of one assertion, of any one opinion. Yet may I not in this be free from sin ? May there not be superior beings, amused with any graceful though instinctive attitude my mind may fall into, as I am entertained with the alertness of the Stoat or the anxiety of the Deer ? Though a quarrel in the streets is a thing to be hated, the energies displayed in it are fine; the commonest Man shows a grace in his quarrel. By a superior Being our reasonings may take the same tone—though erroneous, they may be fine. This is the very thing in which consists Poetry, and if so it is not so fine a thing as philosophy—for the same reason that an eagle is not so fine a thing as a truth. Give me this credit—Do you not think I strive—to know myself ? "

This was the man who died at twenty-five; known to some as " Johnny Keats," and to others as a fine sensual poet of great courage and generous nature. He died in the most distressing circumstances that could well be imagined; and our knowledge of his end has thrown a shadow back over his whole life. But the shadow was not really there; and, until the sudden stroke of his illness, he was a young man of amazingly expanding gifts, full of hope and enthusiasm. It requires some effort to think away the shadow and to surmise what he might have become; and the result induces melancholy.

The Later Poetry of Mr. W. B. Yeats[1]

In his preface to *The Wild Swans at Coole*, Mr. Yeats observes that certain characters " have once again become a part of the phantasmagoria through which I can alone express my convictions about the world "; and, though the misplacement of an adverb makes the sentence a little difficult to follow, it does contain the precise necessary word for which Mr. Yeats's critics, left to themselves, might have sought and sought in vain. A good many writers have been misled by his own belief that in dreams he finds a higher reality or a solution of the problem of reality. He has assumed that he is a mystic; and others have followed him in the assumption.

The two essays of his *Per Amica Silentia Lunae* were written on this assumption, and they raised the question of its justness in an emphatic form. They were very definitely in his own style, full of phrases, sentences, and paragraphs equal to the best in his lyrics, plays, and tales. But the doctrine which they sought to convey appeared on analysis to be derived by second-rate thinking from doubtful intuitions. It was supported by argument and the argument would not bear analysis. It had neither the fire nor the clarity of true mystical apprehension. What these qualities really are can be seen in A. E.'s practical and matter-of-fact treatise, *The Candle of Vision*, which makes a good contrast with *Per Amica Silentia Lunae*. There is, as every one knows, a state between sleeping and

---

[1] *The Wild Swans at Coole.* By W. B. Yeats. (Macmillan.)
Two Plays for Dancers. By W. B. Yeats. (Cuala Press.)

waking—but nearer to sleeping—in which the dreamer imagines himself practising all manner of arts with which he is in reality unfamiliar, from (according to the person) playing the piano to walking on a tight-rope. It must be in some such condition as this that Mr. Yeats imagines himself a mystic philosopher; and the hypothesis is supported by the rather frequent references in his essays to slight trances, visions of the night, and the moments after he has laid his head on the pillow.

Now, by using this excellent word " phantas-magoria," with its inseparable connotations of fantasy and unreality, he confesses that it is out of dream-shapes that he creates beauty, as others create it out of the men and women, the trees and hills and animals that they see in their waking moments. It is a phantasmagoria that he describes in *The Collar-bone of a Hare*:—

" Would I could cast a sail on the water
Where many a king has gone
And many a king's daughter,
And alight at the comely trees and the lawn,
The playing upon pipes and the dancing,
And learn that the best thing is
To change my loves while dancing
And pay but a kiss for a kiss.

I would find by the edge of that water
The collar-bone of a hare
Worn thin by the lapping of water,
And pierce it through with a gimlet and stare
At the old bitter world where they marry in
    churches,
And laugh over the untroubled water
At all who marry in churches,
Through the white bone of a hare."

239

It would be possible, perhaps, to extract from that some comment on life. But this comment, when extracted, would not represent the real meaning of the poem. It is, in the first place and principally, a picture. Mr. Yeats's world, in the fullest sense, the world, that is to say, which gives him the sensations whence his poems proceed, is a dream-world. The events of ordinary life come to him transmuted through that medium and confused with events that have happened only in books or in imagination. The dream-state reduces them all to the same plane of existence. And, whatever may be the origin and the meaning of dreams, they are not to be confused with the transcendent visions of the mystic. Mr. Yeats offers us no precept of life in his poetry, but only a picture of a region of beauty which is peculiarly his own.

Some of his poems, it is true, derive still as always from waking moments, from actual or vicarious experience in the real world. Such, for example, in *The Wild Swans*, is *An Irish Airman Foresees His Death*:—

> " I know that I shall meet my fate
> Somewhere among the clouds above;
> Those that I fight I do not hate,
> Those that I guard I do not love;
> My country is Kiltartan Cross,
> My countrymen Kiltartan's poor,
> No likely end could bring them loss
> Or leave them happier than before.
> Nor law, nor duty bade me fight,
> Nor public man, nor angry crowds,
> A lonely impulse of delight
> Drove to this tumult in the clouds;
> I balanced all, brought all to mind,

> The years to come seemed waste of breath,
> A waste of breath the years behind
> In balance with this life, this death."

The conception of that piece is excellent; and, save in one inept expression, it is characteristic of the strict and economical beauty of Mr. Yeats's later style. But it is by no means characteristic of his mood. His last volume of verse, *Responsibilities*, led some observers to believe that the mood here exemplified was growing more common with him, that he was turning from dreams to ordinary life. They were deceived by a development in his style. For the only serious change that he has undergone since his first appearance is that, whereas he used to depict his dreams in language which had too often the confusion and vagueness of a dream, he now takes care to be wide awake during the act of composition.

He has stripped his diction of most of the pallid, flabby words that took off the edge of ecstasy in his early work and muffled so much of what was best even in *The Wind Among the Reeds*. The objects he describes are less often " dim " or " pale," the words " dream " and " rose " are less monotonously recurrent; and when these words do appear, it is no longer because the poet finds them handy on all occasions, but because they have a definite propriety in that place. The result of this change has been to give his diction a curiously bare and economical quality, which makes it stand to his earlier and more luscious work almost as speech to song. It is indeed in many cases, however it may be intended, a lyrical poetry of a new kind which derives its beauty from the speaking rather than from the singing voice. In the *Two Plays for Dancers* Mr. Yeats brings musicians on the stage and directs them to sing. But the songs he puts in their mouths are like this:—

> " How many centuries spent
> The sedentary soul
> In toils of measurement
> Beyond eagle or mole,
> Beyond hearing or seeing,
> Or Archimedes guess,
> To raise into being
> That loveliness ? "

That needs no music and would hardly admit it. It is, too, in its apparent carelessness and spontaneity, typical of the best of Mr. Yeats's later style, from which the element of formality and pose has been expelled with extraordinary success. His danger lies in allowing himself sometimes to suppose that ease of manner can be attained by mere negligence, as when he writes:—

> " I think it better that in times like these
> A poet keep his mouth shut, for in truth
> We have no gift to set a statesman right."

But here perhaps not only the manner but the theme has been unfortunate. Though he has done it with success on more than one occasion, it is not Mr. Yeats's business to describe the actual world, but to make beautiful pictures out of his dreams. This, whatever may be the origin of their inspiration, he still does in the *Two Plays for Dancers*. These show no very obvious signs of Japanese influence, though their author points proudly to it. There is no scenery, there is a chorus of musicians and the characters wear masks; but these details do not appear greatly to have changed Mr. Yeats's dramatic method. They are phantasmagorias, very difficult to follow, sometimes boring the reader by their shadowiness, sometimes inexplicably enchanting him with rhythm and imagery when he can least understand them. They sometimes also, it is true, bore him by sheer flatness, an unusual fault in Mr. Yeats, but one which is remarkably frequent in these two volumes. But they still contain passages like incantations in which the reader is, as it were, drugged by strong words and pictures. Such is the scene in which the fugitive of Easter Week is guided by the ghosts of Dermot and Dervorgilla, once traitors to Ireland. It is described in an interlude by the First Musician, partly speaking, partly singing:—

" They've passed the shallow well and the flat
    stone
Fouled by the drinking cattle, the narrow lane
Where mourners for five centuries have carried
Noble or peasant to his burial.
An owl is crying out above their heads.
(*Singing*) Why should the heart take fright
What sets it beating so ?
The bitter sweetness of the night
Has made it but a lonely thing.
Red bird of March, begin to crow,
Up with the neck and clap the wing,
Red cock, and crow.

(*They go once round the stage. The First Musician*
    speaks.)

And now they have climbed through the long
    grassy field
And passed the ragged thorn trees and the gap

In the ancient hedge; and the tomb-nested owl
At the foot's level beats with a vague wing.
(*Singing*) My head is in a cloud;
I'd let the whole world go.
My rascal heart is proud
Remembering and remembering.
Red bird of March, begin to crow,
Up with the neck and clap the wing,
Red cock, and crow."

It is easier here to receive an impression from
the whole than to explain the significance of any
of the parts; but inexplicability has always been a
prominent feature in Mr. Yeats's best performances.

W. E. Henley

WILLIAM ERNEST HENLEY died in 1903. To-day
his influence on living literature, though not the
result of it, has almost ceased to exist. " Henley's
young men " have grown up and become their own
masters. Now and again one of them pays him
a resounding compliment; men so diverse as Mr.
H. G. Wells and Mr. W. B. Yeats have testified to
his greatness. His poems continue to be read.
The copy I have before me shows that they were
reprinted at regular intervals seventeen times
between 1898 and 1917. A collected edition of
his works is in course of publication; and the
fourth and penultimate volume [1] has just appeared.
But Henley himself is passing into the legendary
state. If you mentioned him to the young writers
of to-day, his name would have no particular effect
on them. If you were to analyse the influences that
are helping to mould modern literature and to point
out the precursors of its chief strains, his name
would hardly appear in your essay. The sweet
war-man is not dead and rotten; but his ghost
has not so powerful an arm as the living swash-
buckler.

Henley in part created, in part was affected by,
an attitude towards the world which nowadays we
have replaced by another. Stevenson asked, " Shall
we never shed blood ? "; and Henley thought it
would be a pity if we never did. For him any blood
was better than none, even that which is shed when
one bruiser hits another on the nose. When

[1] *Views and Reviews.* By W. E. Henley. (Macmillan.)

Henley and Stevenson collaborated as dramatists the heroes of three out of their four plays were respectively a deacon who was also a house-breaker, the ex-captain of a slaver, and the celebrated criminal, Robert Macaire. Henley's prologue to *Admiral Guinea* begins with the lines—

> " Once was an Age, an Age of blood and gold,
>   An Age of shipmen scoundrelly and bold. . . ."

But Stevenson's inquiry expressed a more than half-whimsical frame of mind; and in these plays he contrived that a purely whimsical love of horrors should prevail. Henley, however, was in dead earnest. He wrote in *The Song of the Sword*:—

> " Black and lean, gray and cruel,
>   Short-hilted, long-shafted,
>   I froze into steel;
>   And the blood on my elder,
>   His hand on the hafts of me,
>   Sprang like a wave——"

The twentieth-century commentary on that was to be seen in the umbrella-stands of many English homes during the war. There stood swords (at four guineas each) whose owners were at the front, fighting with bombs and loaded sticks. But Henley believed in his sword, and many of his associates believed with him. They agitated for the return of adventure to the world; and Mr. Kipling was of the party. It was a rebellion against the sedentary life and environment of the ordinary English citizen and the ordinary English writer; but, because it was not quite spontaneous, because it was for the most part a mere reaction against something else, it tended too often to confuse adventure and violence, eloquence and shouting, strength and brutality. It was born largely in the brain, not in the feelings, not in a natural necessity, and having sometimes but the feeblest of roots in genuine conviction it was liable to express itself in a vehemence which bordered on hysteria. There is no doubting where it came from; it was one of the many products of Darwinism, as Henley's sword makes clear when it sings of

> " Sifting the nations,
> The slag from the metal,
> The waste and the weak
> From the fit and the strong."

But cooler reflection suggests that man, if he is the highest result of evolution, may, perhaps, be able to refine, for his own purposes, on nature's crude process. And we have learnt that bloodshed on the largest scale is almost ludicrously easy to arrange, and that, considering it on the lowest plane, it may be the dullest of occupations. Henley's reaction against softness and the sedentary life is always possible and may always have salutary effects. But the mode of that reaction is, for this generation at least, and perhaps for many generations to follow it, quite impossible. If we engage in bloodshed again we are not likely to be reinforced by an abstract love of it for its own sake.

Henley's doctrine, in its extreme form, was intellectual, not a genuine outcome of his whole spiritual being; and the fault which it bred in his writing was the fault bred by all not quite genuine convictions, namely, rhetoric. Rhetoric, in the bad sense, means, I suppose, a form of expression which exceeds the feeling to be expressed. In one of the best essays in *Views and Review*, Henley defines with extraordinary delicacy and rightness the qualities of Mr. Austin Dobson's poetry:—

" The epithet is usually so just that it seems to have come into being with the noun it qualifies; the metaphor is mostly so appropriate that it leaves you in doubt as to whether it suggested the poem or the poem suggested it; the verb is never in excess of the idea it would convey; the effect of it all is that " something has here got itself uttered," and for good."

He quotes a passage and continues: " The words I have italicised are the only words (it seems) in the language that are proper to the occasion: and yet how quietly they are produced, with what apparent unconsciousness they are set to do their work, how just and how sufficient is their effect! " This is praise which Henley himself never deserved and never can receive. " The verb is never in excess of the idea that it would convey." He has written a description of a poet who is anything but rhetorical; and in doing so he has described his own antithesis. Let us take what is perhaps his own best known poem:—

" Out of the night that covers me,
　　Black as the Pit from pole to pole,
　I thank whatever gods may be
　　For my unconquerable soul.

　. . . It matters not how strait the gate,
　　How charged with punishment the scroll,
　I am the master of my fate;
　　I am the captain of my soul."

248

It is fine; but is one not conscious that almost every phrase, by however narrow a degree, is " in excess of the idea it would convey " ? It is not discreet, it is not modest, and in poetry discretion and modesty are of the essence of true strength. Henley's poetry was frequently fine. There are in it elements of vigour, sincerity, and freshness; but almost all of it is vitiated by an insincere violence of expression. And when he forsakes violence, it is for sentimentality:—

> " This is the moon of roses,
>   The lovely and flowerful time;
> And as white roses climb the wall,
>   Your dreams about me climb."

No doubt there is an emotion here; but it is smothered under an exaggerated languishing, under an inexact diction, which make it seem like one of the usual bad translations of Heine. When a house is built on sand it does not matter what excellence of design, what value of material, or what earnestness of purpose goes to the building. It will eventually disappear; and Henley's poetry will disappear.

But Henley remains. He is that not altogether unparalleled phenomenon, a great figure in literature who is not a great writer. Dr. Johnson is the chief exemplar of his class. Of course, Johnson was a very much better writer than Henley; and if he had been nothing else he would still have survived, as Henley would not. But if Johnson's name meant nothing more to us than the *Lives of the Poets*, *Rasselas*, and the *Vanity of Human Wishes*, it would not be, as it is, one of the five or six first thought of in the history of English letters. Henley, like

Johnson, was more important for what he was than for what he did; his misfortune, and ours, lies in the fact that he had no biographer. There are many legends about him. We know all about his eagerness and his vehemence and his loud voice; but there is no single portrait of him which gives the truth and nothing less than the truth. His sayings and his opinions are scattered in the memories of some dozens of men, and now, perhaps, will never be collected. The best of him is contained in this volume of *Views and Reviews,* where are collected the journalistic articles he wrote for one paper or another in the ordinary pursuit of his profession. In these he was more nearly his natural self than in any of his more ambitious attempts; and it is possible to see more clearly here than elsewhere the natural vigour and simplicity of his style, the natural masculinity and directness of his judgment. His essays on Disraeli, Hugo, Arnold, and Tennyson are masterpieces of insight and lucid expression; and the whole book shows that soundness and strength, combined with readableness, the casual writer on literary subjects may attain. But his chief importance lies elsewhere than in his merit as a critic. He was sometimes a stimulating writer; but he was always a stimulating personality, and, above all, a stimulating editor. He induced young men to write, and, by bullying or whatever other method suggested itself, he forced them to write well. He would have thought this, perhaps, not so satisfactory as being a great poet; but he might have been twice as good a poet and yet never have reached the commanding position which, when his books are forgotten and his ideas fail even to arouse any resentment, he must continue to hold.

Mr. Rabindranath Tagore

AFTER reading the memoirs of almost any writer above or below the level of mere mediocrity, one is inclined to exclaim that such books are the most interesting in the world. Most readers have an inexhaustible appetite for them, as is proved by the public which eagerly swallows the most insipid volumes of reminiscences. There is no nonsense about them; you can base theories on them. For either the author is making confession or you can suspect him of being a liar; and either hypothesis flatters equally our pride in our judgment of humanity. But Mr. Rabindranath Tagore's memoirs [1] have a double value. They can be read for themselves alone and they can also be read for the purpose of forming a more definite idea of a writer whom we do not yet perfectly understand. He has been taken down whole by a more or less intelligent public, but criticism has not yet done with him. It has been decided, perhaps, that he is of importance, but not how important he is or in what way, or whether in English he may not be more of a curiosity than a poet. This volume, therefore, apart from the fact that it consists of confessions, is valuable because it furnishes more useful materials for a correct judgment than we have had hitherto.

One thing emerges at once very definitely. Tagore is not the latest voice of an ancient, classical and independent literature, as some of us were led by his first sponsors to suppose; he does not convey a snub from the long-civilised East to the

[1] *My Reminiscences.* By Sir Rabindranath Tagore. (Macmillan.)

lately barbarous West. It is quite clear from his story that he has seen the creation of modern Bengali literature in his own time, that he stands to it himself (if we may accept his presumed greatness) much as Goethe stood to German literature, and that, like Goethe, he owes a very significant debt to the writers of this country. He says in one passage:—

" Shortly after, as I added to my years, I attained a place as the youngest of the literary men of the time; but what was to be my position in order of merit was not even then settled. The little reputation I had acquired was mixed with plenty of doubt and not a little of condescension. It was then the fashion in Bengal to assign each man of letters a place in comparison with a supposed compeer in the West. Thus one was the Byron of Bengal, another the Emerson, and so forth. I began to be styled by some the Bengal Shelley. This was insulting to Shelley and only likely to get me laughed at."

Such comparisons as these are not made in a settled literature with a firm tradition of its own Belgian literature was a comparatively new and unstable conception when M. Maeterlinck was called the " Belgian Shakespeare." The conclusion to be drawn is not doubtful. But Mr. Tagore also indicates here the fact that the Bengal of his youth was a place of great literary excitement and commotion. It is a little difficult to disentangle the artistic and poetical achievements of his six elder brothers, but one of them at least—the eldest— was the author of a work called *The Dream Journey*, which Mr. Tagore describes with enthusiasm as one of the Bengali classics. Another invented and bravely wore a national costume for all India, which combined the practical advantages of Western tailoring with the grace and dignity of Eastern drapery. It would be interesting to see it. His cousins were equally exuberant; and the whole of the second half of this book is a record of literary friendships and discipleships, foundations of Academies and publications of critical reviews. It ends, unfortunately, in the author's early twenties, and does not tell us how the ferment became more and more productive and how he himself established and developed his reputation. But it goes far enough to show the conditions under which his youth was passed and the influences which formed his talent.

He looks back, like every other poet who has gone through a period of this sort, and distinguishes between the circumstances that were useful to him and those which hurt him. The comparison between the positions of the young Goethe in Germany and the young Tagore in Bengal has already been made. But if we put his reflections side by side with those expressed by Goethe in *Dichtung und Wahrheit*, it is a contrast that we find. Goethe complained that he and his friends received no guidance and were left to create German literature without the restraint of useful criticism; Tagore speaks with much gratitude of his elders and his masters. He generously owns his indebtedness to many—to Bankim Babu, who paid a splendid compliment to his first successful book; to Akshay Babu, " who had made the passion in English literature living to us "; and to Rajendrahal, the President of the *Sahitza Parishat* (Academy of Literature).

First Essays on Literature

The impression left in the mind by this part of the book is that of a generation suddenly awaking to literary consciousness and proceeding in a great hurry in moods varying from self-confidence to complete reliance on foreign models. The account which Tagore gives of his own poetical growth is not so clear or so vivid. He writes throughout with a sort of half-humorous self-depreciation that is, no doubt, morally commendable, but which ends by getting on the reader's nerves. His comments on poetry in general, however, are always interesting, as when he says:—

" I tried to make out (in a lecture) that to bring out better what the words sought to express was the chief end and aim of vocal music. . . . But I must make the confession to-day that the opinion I voiced with such enthusiasm that evening was wrong. The art of vocal music has its own special functions and features. And when it happens to be set to words the latter must not presume too much on their opportunity and seek to supersede the melody of which they are but the vehicle. The song being great in its own wealth, why should it wait upon the words ? Rather does it begin where mere words fail. Its power lies in the region of the inexpressible; it tells us what the words cannot. . . . So the less a song is burdened with words the better. . . . In Bengal, however, the words have always asserted themselves, so that our provincial song has failed to develop her full musical capabilities and has remained content as the handmaiden of her sister art of poetry. . . . I have often felt this while composing my songs. As I hummed to myself and wrote the lines. . . . I found that the words had no means of reaching by themselves the region into which they were borne away by the tune."

This is a valuable opinion from a practitioner of a literature which has not, like our own, decreed a divorce between music and poetry. Possibly it is wrong, and Tagore's youthful judgment was right; but his considered opinion is stimulating and might provoke endless discussions on a difficult and vital question.

So much for this interesting book looked at by itself—but we think its peculiar importance lies in the fact that it gives that last touch to the picture derived from the works already made available in English which throws the whole into a proper perspective. It shows Tagore to be, not a typical figure, *the* Eastern or Indian poet, but *a* Bengali poet and a member, moreover, of a generation which learnt largely and eagerly from English literature. When he appeared as a representative of the East he caused some disappointment by being insufficiently Oriental; or else his admirers made themselves look foolish by discovering in him Oriental traits which were not there or were long familiar in English poetry. His reputation was liable to suffer either way. There is a story which is told of a dinner given to Tagore by a company of English admirers. One of them, after the meal, cried, " Master, will you not sing us one of your mystical songs ? " Thereupon the Master, in whom ignorant adulation had not destroyed a sense of humour, folded his hands and cast up his eyes and sang, while the English disciples swooned with awe, one of the rollicking and broadly comic drinking-songs which he wrote in his youth. There never was much Eastern mystery in Tagore; but

255

so long as his readers looked for it and failed to find it, they were puzzled and more than half-inclined to suspect a deeper mystery than ever. But there is nothing more extraordinary in the entry of Bengali into the company of modern literature than there was in the entry of Russian.

It is not until we cease to look in Tagore for a poet different in kind from our own poets that we can expect to appreciate him justly; and this just appreciation will not now be long delayed. We must learn first to understand that his vision and his methods of expressing it are not wholly alien from those to which we are accustomed; but that he is a poet of a particular sort and not the general interpreter of a whole people. Those who called him the Shelley of Bengal were not very exact epigrammatists; but their heads were at least pointed in the right direction. It is as foolish to read Tagore keeping in mind all the time the fact that he is an Indian, as it would be to read Shelley against a persistent background of the fact that he was born in Sussex. Tagore is vaguely like Shelley in that he is more occupied with emotions than with persons, with thoughts than with things. He tends, that is to say, to dwell on matters that are common to all humanity; and he lacks, in consequence, the vivid local colour that has rather idiotically been expected of him.

This appears quite plainly in the pleasant first half of the present volume, a simple narrative from which no other moral can be drawn. The circumstances of Tagore's childhood did, of course, differ widely from those of an English childhood. Nevertheless many of his experiences at school with the masters and with the other boys would hardly be out of place in a Western setting; and the adventure of his mind during his early years were such as must be common to imaginative children all over the world. But, even taking into consideration the fact that Tagore is here writing for an Indian and not a European audience, it would be impossible to avoid noticing that very little stress is thrown on local circumstances. The poet is more interested in the thoughts and feelings of the child than in his surroundings; and the local colour might almost have been within the powers of an English novelist who had never been in India. However this may be, it is a faithful and pleasing picture of a little boy; and it will immediately appear so to those who are able to approach it with an open mind and without any absurd craving for a bizarre setting.

Sweet Bodements

NOVELS about the future, which are a comparatively recent development in imaginative literature, are probably the descendants of the old Utopia. Formerly, a writer who desired to encourage his fellows by picturing ideal life or mock them by exaggerating or inventing their peculiarities, needed only to be blown from his course by a storm which lasted six days and six nights and carried away the instruments of navigation. It was then easy to sight an unknown island, whose natives practised community of goods or propagation by fissure or whatever the writer might wish to urge as a remedy for the evils of civilisation. This was still possible late in the nineteenth century, when Hertzka made his *Reise nach Freiland* and Higgins crossed the ranges into Erewhon. But geographical discovery, which some persons erroneously believe to have taken romance from the earth, did close this avenue of invention to the romancer. The last Utopia of note was that of Mr. Wells; and here the author had to confess that he could not be satisfied with an island so small as not to have been noticed or a narrow country behind an unspecified mountain-range. Nothing less than a world was enough, and accordingly he invented a world.

But this device has not been copied. The imaginative writer is often curiously bound by matters of fact. He can invent a small island or a tribe of talking monkeys hidden in Africa, but commonly he shirks imagining an unknown island in the Pacific large enough to hold a highly developed community. This is because he knows

258

too well that there is no such thing, and perhaps the doubt whether life exists elsewhere or the difficulty of removing his characters from the earth prevents him from following Mr. Wells's example. He is consequently thrown forward into the future. There must be, after all, a future of some sort, and relying on this indubitable truth, many novelists have disported themselves therein during the last twenty or thirty years. The collection and examination of their works, and the comparison of their ideas, make an agreeable side-issue in literature which, so far as I know, has not been explored by any amateur of such curiosities.

It offers a huge field to collector and student. My own collection, both tangible and mental, is large, but it cannot include half the existing specimens. Many which I have seen—some of them books by cranks, worthless as literature or speculation, yet perhaps to the collector the most interesting of all—lie still where I happened to read them, before the fancy for such a collection took me. In some cases, I have forgotten both author and title, and only tantalising scraps of detail still remind me of books which are now hard to trace. Fortunately, I do not intend making an exhaustive study of the subject; but I recommend it to any one seeking a theme for an academic essay, in which he may agreeably combine literature, sociological speculation, and the psychology of the mildly imbecile. He will find all that and more in any adequate collection of these books, and I shall be happy to give him any assistance I can, wishing, as one so often does, to read a treatise I lack the industry to write.

The second difficulty which meets the student when he has roughly surveyed the field of inquiry is that of definition. This seems at first sight easier than it is in reality. I have before me now a recent publication, *The Apostle of the Cylinder*, by Mr. Victor Rousseau, which corresponds well to the vague conceptions suggested by the term " a novel about the future." The hero is shut into a cylinder designed to preserve him in suspended animation, as biologists actually can preserve fragments of living tissue. He returns to life in 2014, in a world which, shattered by successive revolutions, has organised itself scientifically and divided its population into a small ruling class of " normals " and various grades of " defectives," whose matings are strictly regulated. The purpose of the book is mainly satirical, but it contains much good incidental detail, as in the discovery of two new colours in the spectrum, " mull, below red, and glow, above violet." The satirical intention is in strict relation with reality. One might not believe in the evolution of a State in which the population was classified by cranial measurements and reaction tests and had its activities restricted accordingly. But soon after reading this book, I read also a report of an address delivered before the Royal Medical Society by a certain scientist who is a distinguished man, but who appears to be (if I may use the term without offence) a typical defective of a type not yet recognised by his colleagues. He is defective, that is to say, in humour, common sense, and humanity; for on this occasion he advocated the retention of compulsory medical grading after the war on the ground that women would tend to " mate " (he might, in the circumstances, have used a nakeder phrase) only with the higher grades. Since there are really men whose minds function in this way, Mr. Rousseau's inventions cannot be dismissed as

mere fantasy. His parody of scientific " thinking "
is excellent, if rather bitter, fooling. In this book,
the broken world clings to science as its shield
against disaster, and science rapidly assumes a
pontifical place:—

" World councils of scientists laid down the
dogmas of universal knowledge in the Vienna
Creed, which was adopted without dissentients,
after those who objected had been put to death.
The famous quarrel whether Force is of the same
substance as Matter, or a like substance, was
decided here. The Sames conquered the Similars,
by virtue of a proclamation from Boss Rose."

Later on, a version of the Vienna Creed is given:—

" I believe in Science Supreme, and Force and
Matter, co-existent and consubstantial, according to
the Vienna Creed, and in the Boss, the Keeper of
Knowledge. That man dies as the beast dies.
And that we are immortal in the germ-plasm,
through our descendants. I believe in Darwin,
Hæckel, and Wells, who brought us to enlighten-
ment. . . ."

This is all well invented, and the climax, in which
science is overthrown by the resurgent forces of
humanity, relieves the mind and gladdens the
heart.

I have described Mr. Rousseau's book at length,
not only because it is good, but also because it is a
specimen about which there can be no doubt. But
it is not always so easy to decide whether any given
story is admissible. A book in which the action is

dated later than the year of writing is not necessarily eligible. We need not concern ourselves, for example, with political novels which begin in 1925 in order to make easy the introduction of an imaginary Prime Minister, nor are we concerned with Jules Verne's submarine, which did not much affect the fate of the world. But there are innumerable border-line cases which seriously perplex me. I am not sure whether Mr. Wells's *Food of the Gods* is to be classified as a single fantastic incident or not. There is one book, prophesying the union of the Churches, which I treasure, but which causes me grave doubts. (I like it chiefly because of a Catholic priest in it, who finds one of his flock reading a book which is on the Index, and tells her that he will " have to speak to the Holy Father about excommunicating her.") Perhaps the desired phenomenon may be defined as a novel, the action of which takes place at some date later than the present, and which reveals the social order substantially changed, either by evolution or by a single catastrophe.

This leaves us a wide range, in the examination of which many curious facts appear. One interesting point is that the nearer the prophet gets to the end of the race or the world, the more poetical he becomes. Mr. Wells's *Time Machine*, which ventures into remote futurity, is much more a product of the imagination than his ingenious *The Sleeper Wakes*, which goes only a paltry couple of centuries. It is true that his " time traveller " finds many thousands of years hence a definite comment on our own social order in the feeble, pretty, childish descendants of the privileged classes who dwell above ground and are preyed on by the ferocious, though etiolated, Morlocks, the descendants of our proletariat, who dwell underground and eat the flesh of their late masters. But even this episode is poetically described; and the next, when the traveller goes farther and arrives on the gray beach of a desolate ocean and sees large crabs crawling about in the cold air, under a failing sun, has a strong imaginative quality. Flecker's *Last Generation* shows the ultimate survivors of a voluntarily sterilised generation, huddling together in a dismantled world and watching the invasion of gray apes, who, even as the last men, in the agony of death, observe them, discover the art of making fire. This is a conception worthy of the poet who formed it. In *The Purple Cloud*, Mr. M. P. Shiel describes the extinction of the race, save for an explorer who happily chanced to be at the North Pole and a Turkish girl-baby walled up in a cellar, by a poison-cloud of volcanic origin. Mr. Shiel's book, which appeared many years ago in a magazine, and was promptly forgotten, is one of the best of its kind extant, and will bear examination apart from its kind, for it rises with its wealth of imagery and fantastic passion to the level of its extraordinary theme. There is also a French book by M. Rosny, which is at least original if its details are rather too mechanically invented. Here the earth has become a desert (in complete contradiction of the latest geological theories [1]), and the few survivors of mankind live in oases round the last springs, which are at the mercy of seismic disturbances and vanish one by one. But a new form of life has appeared, a race which the author calls *les ferro-magnetaux*, and which I visualise (they are not very clearly described)

---

[1] Four years have elapsed since this was written. I no longer know what the latest geological theories may be, but my parenthesis may be presumed to be now out of date.

as a kind of animated rust, a sort of metallic alternative to protoplasm. They are the race of the future, and they devour (by absorbing the blood in an obscure and unconvincing manner) humans who are so unwary as to sleep in the desert. When the last man finds that no water is left and that death is inevitable, he goes into the desert and offers himself as prey in order that his life may pass into that of the new race. This is a fine end, but the whole book is rather arid and devoid of poetry. The most poetic of all this class is, of course, Mr. W. H. Hudson's lovely *Crystal Age*, an age in which mankind dwells in a few widely separated patriarchal households, beautiful and long-lived, simple, infinitely wise, and in constant communion with the earth. But this is so far out of relation with anything that could reasonably be prophesied that it is rather, perhaps, a fairy-tale than a book about the future—one step further from reality than Morris's real "earthly paradise." It is like, however, *News from Nowhere*, a story from which one rises with the gloom of daily life momentarily deepened.

Satirical visions of the future are rarely very good. They are too often written by people who are mainly anti-something or other; and people of that stamp are infrequently intelligent. Mr. Rousseau's book is an exception; but its satire is presented in a very serious way. There is another and more impressive exception in the last section of the *Ile des Pingouins* which sets out the future of mankind with an ironical and terrible gaiety. This section is called *L'Histoire sans Fin*. Its first paragraph begins: " On ne trouvait jamais les maisons assez hautes; on les surélevait sans cesse, et l'on en construisit de trente à quarante étages. . . ."

And so it goes, through destruction and ruin, to a new growth of " la civilisation pingouine"; and the last paragraph begins: " Elle s'enrichit et s'acessit démesurément. On ne trouvait jamais les maisons assez hautes. . . ."

What one might call the " middle future " is, of course, the happy hunting-ground of the crank, who imagines the most marvellous and the most diverting mechanical improvements. In one book, the memory of which I cherish, though not, alas, the memory of its title or its author, the hero is a great scientist, who, having produced a human being by chemical processes, announces his intention of thus largely increasing the output, and is astonished (the author sympathetically astonished and hurt with him) when his reactionary fellow-citizens look on the project with disfavour. But all, mad or sane, are, curiously, almost unanimous in the opinion that applied science will continue in the future at its present rate of progress. This is not questioned by Mr. Wells (save in one instance) or Mr. Rousseau or Monsignor Benson in his two pictures of an Atheist and a Catholic future. (You pay your six shillings and have the opportunity of finding either alternative as uninviting as the other. Certain items of " progress "—for example, moving pavements, gramophone newspapers, and legalised and organised suicide (sometimes called euthanasy)— frequently occur, and development on such lines, for good or evil, appears to be the common anticipation. Yet, I suppose, the reverse is at least possible. It is sketched in Mr. Wells's *War in the Air*, where the ravages of battle leave the whole world keeping pigs, without its heritage of science; but the description is not carried far enough. Much the same state is reached in Jack London's *The Scarlet*

Plague, but here the population is reduced to, I think, one in thirty millions, and this should perhaps be classed as an " end of the race book " rather than as a vision of the middle future. Richard Jefferies did it rather more elaborately in *After London* by means of an obscure astronomical disaster which considerably altered the configuration of the earth; but, save for a few good passages in which he described wild nature resuming its supremacy over the garden-like English countryside, and an extraordinarily vivid picture of London deserted and become a pestilential swamp, he plunged the world so deep into a new Dark Age that he might just as well have been writing about the original Dark Ages. His characters were feudal barons, who fought one another with bows and arrows, catapults and battering-rams; and except that they smoked cigars, grown in Devonshire, it is hard to see how they differ from their prototypes. What I should like to see is a book showing our present civilisation sinking gradually into decay, not hurried there by some single cataclysm, but rather falling nation by nation to the state of the less satisfactory South American republics and below it, from causes as much or as little explicable as those that withdrew genius from Athens, undermined the Roman Empire, and stopped the spirit of Gothic in mediæval Europe. I can conceive several chains of events which might lead—plausibly enough at least for a novel—to such a result; for example, a balance between capital and labour, each determined to subdue the other, and neither quite strong enough to manage it. It is arguable that our science is too permanently secured in books ever to be quite lost, though, as Mr. Belloc has pointed out, there must have been a great wealth of Roman technical

266

literature which has utterly disappeared. But this possibility is not strong enough to stand in the way of writing such a novel; and, if some ingenious author would give six months or so of his time to it, I should have a notable piece to add to my collection. It is, in fact, one of the books which I should dearly like to see some one else write—but which I am damned if I will write myself.[1]

[1] I leave this sentence unchanged—but I regret to own that I have now made myself liable to the damnation I so rashly invoked.